W9-ASR-331

Reforming Private Health Insurance

Mark A. Hall

The AEI Press

Publisher for the American Enterprise Institute
WASHINGTON, D.C.

1994

Library of Congress Cataloging-in-Publication Data

Hall, Mark A.
    Reforming private health insurance / Mark A. Hall.
      p.   cm.
    Includes index.
    ISBN 0-8447-3862-X. — ISBN 0-8447-3863-8 (pbk.)
    1. Insurance, Health—United States.   I. Title.
HG9396.H322   1994
368.3'82'00973—dc20   94-14779
                                  CIP

3 5 7 9 10 8 6 4 2

© 1994 by the American Enterprise Institute for Public Policy Research, Washington, D.C. All rights reserved. No part of this publication may be used or reproduced in any manner whatsoever without permission in writing from the American Enterprise Institute except in the case of brief quotations embodied in news articles, critical articles, or reviews. The views expressed in the publications of the American Enterprise Institute are those of the authors and do not necessarily reflect the views of the staff, advisory panels, officers, or trustees of AEI.

Printed in the United States of America

368.382
H17

95-2259
30110763

Contents

CONTENTS

Acknowledgment

I am grateful for the financial support of the American Enterprise Institute and the guidance provided by Robert Helms. This book is based in part on earlier work sponsored by the Robert Wood Johnson Foundation: Mark A. Hall, "Reforming the Health Insurance Market for Small Businesses," *New England Journal of Medicine*, vol. 326 (1992), pp. 565–70, and Mark A. Hall, "The Political Economics of Health Insurance Market Reform," *Health Affairs*, vol. 11, no. 2 (Summer 1992), pp. 108–24.

I am indebted to many persons for helping me understand the mysteries of private health insurance, especially to Rick Curtis and Kevin Haugh, formerly at the Health Insurance Association of America and now with the Institute for Health Policy Solutions. This work would not have been possible without their many insights. The opinions and conclusions expressed in this book are solely my own, however.

1
Introduction

Something is terribly wrong with the health insurance market. After a half-century of rapid-to-steady growth, private health insurance is now said to be in a "death spiral." Employers are dropping insurance at an alarming rate. In 1989 twice as many firms added insurance coverage as dropped it; in 1990 and 1991 the opposite was true. In recent years, about 10 percent of previously insured firms have dropped coverage each year, while less than half as many firms have become newly insured. Most of this activity has occurred in small firms (fewer than twenty-five employees) or in medium-sized firms (twenty-five to ninety-nine employees).[1] As a consequence, the portion of the population covered by private insurance declined precipitously during the 1980s—from 81 percent of the total population to 70–75 percent (depending on assumptions made about multiple coverage from different sources).[2] This rate of decay is even more rapid for small groups and individuals. The percentage of the population covered by individually purchased health insurance fell by 40 percent between 1987 and 1991 (see figure 1–1),[3] and Families USA estimates that 2 million Americans continue to lose their health insurance coverage each month.

The instability of the health insurance market is also seen in the rising costs for those who have retained coverage. Over the past few years, employers' costs for private insurance have increased from 15 to 20 percent most years, much faster than the increase in total health care spending. According to a survey by a benefits consultant of its

---

1. Cynthia B. Sullivan, Marianne Miller, and Claudia C. Johnson, "Employer-sponsored Health Insurance in 1991" (Washington, D.C.: Health Insurance Association of America, 1992).

2. Randall R. Bovbjerg, Charles C. Griffin, and Caitlin Carroll, "U.S. Health Care Coverage and Costs: Historical Development and Choices for the 1990s," *Journal of Law, Medicine and Ethics*, vol. 21, no. 2 (1993), pp. 141–72.

3. Katharine R. Levit, Gary L. Olin, and Suzanne W. Letsch, "Americans' Health Insurance, 1980–1991," *Health Care Financing Review*, vol. 14, no. 1 (Fall 1992), pp. 31–57.

FIGURE 1–1

PORTION OF TOTAL U.S. POPULATION COVERED BY PRIVATE HEALTH
INSURANCE, 1950–1992
(percent)

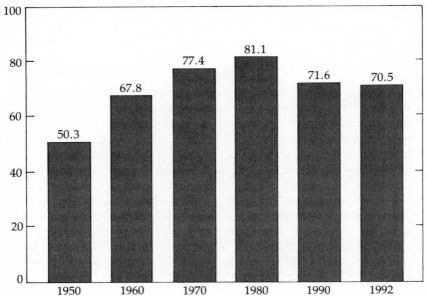

NOTES: For 1990 and later, the table omits hospital indemnity coverages (for example, paying $100 a day during hospital stays), which are typically bought from commercial companies to supplement other coverage. They were included in previous years. In 1990, 14.3 million people (5.7 percent of the population) had such coverage. Including them would raise the net percentage covered to the extent that these indemnity purchasers did not have other coverage.
SOURCES: Cynthia B. Sullivan, Marianne Miller, and Claudia C. Johnson, *Employer-Sponsored Health Insurance in 1991* (Washington, D.C.: Health Insurance Association of America, 1992); U.S. Bureau of the Census, *Statistical Abstract of the United States 1992* (Washington, D.C.: Government Printing Office, 1991); Randall R. Bovbjerg, Charles C. Griffin, and Caitlin Carroll, "U.S. Health Care Coverage and Costs," *Journal of Law, Medicine and Ethics* (1993).

clients, the amount employers paid for health care doubled between 1987 and 1992.[4] At the same time, workers' share of health insurance and health care costs is skyrocketing, with a large majority of employers raising their employees' share of the premium and, at the same

4. Foster Higgins study, reported in *American Health Line*, January 27, 1993.

time, increasing deductibles and copayments or decreasing benefits.[5] Many workers complain that what little wage increase they receive each year is entirely absorbed by increases in the cost of health benefits, a complaint that is corroborated by research findings.[6] Although costs increased much less in 1993, they still rose at twice the rate of general inflation.

Despite the tendency to make insurers the scapegoats for these increasing costs, spiraling premiums are not the result of insurance company price gouging. In recent years, many large insurers have consistently lost money or barely broken even on their health insurance products,[7] and several health insurers have gone bankrupt. Even the once invincible Blues (Blue Cross and Blue Shield) have been shaken by financial troubles.

The national concern over the health insurance market is reflected in the barrage of recent state legislation attempting to shore it up. Since 1991, all but four states have enacted significant legislation that affects the pricing or marketing of private health insurance, and well over half the states have enacted fundamental market reforms. If successful, these reforms will prevent further decay in the portion of the market they address (usually small-employer groups), but they will probably not produce a measurable decrease in the number of uninsured Americans or in the rampant growth of health care spending. Achieving these goals will require fundamental reform at the federal level.

Many politicians, academics, and others believe strongly that private insurance should be abandoned in favor of nationalized health

---

See also Walton Francis, "A Health Care Program Run by the Federal Government That Works," *The American Enterprise*, vol. 4, no. 4 (July/August 1993), p. 55, which reports Hay/Huggins survey data showing an average annual increase in private insurance premiums during the 1980s of nearly 14 percent; and Marilyn J. Field and Harold T. Shapiro, eds., *Employment and Health Benefits: A Connection at Risk* (Washington, D.C.: Institute of Medicine, National Academy Press, 1993), p. 109, which reports on HIAA surveys showing 14–20 percent increases for employer premiums each year from 1989 to 1991.

5. Norma Harris, "Employees Are Paying More for Health Benefits," *Business & Health*, July 1993.

6. Michael A. Morrisey, "Mandating Benefits and Compensating Differentials—Taxing the Uninsured," in Robert B. Helms, ed., *American Health Policy: Critical Issues for Reform* (Washington, D.C.: AEI Press, 1993), pp. 135–51; Congressional Budget Office, "Economic Implications of Rising Health Care Costs" (Washington, D.C.: Government Printing Office, October 12, 1992).

7. John K. Iglehart, "The American Health Care System: Private Insurance," *New England Journal of Medicine*, vol. 326 (1992), pp. 1715–20.

insurance, like that in Canada. Most federal lawmakers from both political parties, however, want to preserve and rehabilitate the central role of private insurance. Indeed, private insurance may become even more prominent than it was in its heyday if Medicaid or Medicare is absorbed into the mechanism for delivering health insurance to workers and their families. I will not attempt to resolve this debate, but only observe that, despite all the problems of the private health insurance market, it still has some perceived virtues. Starting from the premise that the United States will, rightly or wrongly, continue to rely for some time on private financing for health care, this volume inquires how to put the health insurance market to best use.

This book begins by explaining why insurance of any sort exists and what social benefits are to be expected from private health insurance. It then surveys the causes of the disintegration of the private insurance market in recent years. Next, it articulates what benefits society can derive from a properly functioning market in health insurance. The bulk of the analysis then explores various proposals to reform the health insurance market, distinguishing broadly between reforms to the existing voluntary system, in which the purchase of insurance is optional, and insurance market reform under a system of mandatory universal coverage of the sort being proposed under the rubric of managed competition.

The portion of this analysis that explores ways to fix the health insurance market is decidedly not prescriptive. It does not attempt to lay out a single comprehensive reform proposal, with many detailed components that accomplish the full range of public policy objectives. Instead, it focuses on common elements in many of the existing proposals that relate to how health insurance should be priced and marketed. The aim of this study is to improve our understanding of the inherent complexities of a private health insurance market, the details of the corrections that are being attempted, and the problems and prospects we are likely to encounter from each variation.

My sources of information are largely eclectic, analytical, and anecdotal rather than rigorously empirical. The health insurance market, because it is private and fragmented, has not been studied as comprehensively as the centralized Medicare program. The great variety of reforms being implemented in the states are too recent to have achieved full effect or to have been carefully evaluated. Necessarily, then, this analysis and its conclusions are somewhat speculative. Nevertheless, the many reliable sources of information that are available shed considerable light on this complex social problem.

2

The Economic and Social Characteristics of Health Insurance

Economists have a clear and precise but somewhat esoteric explanation of why anyone would want to purchase private insurance and, more critically, why we purchase insurance against some risks and not others. This theoretical insight is necessary to understand the social role of private health insurance.[1]

Why Insurance?

Most people dislike risk. In economic terminology, they are risk averse rather than risk neutral or risk takers. Risk-averse people, if given the choice, prefer to avoid, minimize, or shift the risk of suffering a loss, even if doing so has a significant cost. The peace of mind that comes from feeling protected against a loss is capable of carrying a price in private markets, just as more tangible economic goods do. Insurance is an economic vehicle for risk reduction.

Mechanisms other than pure insurance also reduce risk. Investing in loss prevention, either at an individual or societal level, reduces risks. Houses can be made safer from fire and burglary, speed limits can be reduced and highways improved, and income can be saved to protect against disability or death that would leave dependents without support. These actions, which are substitutes for homeowner's,

1. The following account draws from a wide variety of sources, including Susan Feigenbaum, "Risk Bearing in Health Care Finance," in Carl J. Shramm, ed., *Health Care and Its Costs* (New York: W. W. Norton 1987); Kenneth S. Abraham, "Efficiency and Fairness in Insurance Risk Classification," *Virginia Law Review*, vol. 71 (1985), pp. 403–51; Marilyn J. Field and Harold T. Shapiro, *Employment and Health Benefits: A Connection at Risk* (Washington, D.C.: Institute of Medicine; National Academy Press, 1993), pp. 44–47.

automobile, life, and disability insurance, entail private and social costs. Home improvements cost their owner money, people like to drive fast, and those who save money cannot spend it.

Because of these costs, people prefer to reduce a number of risks by shifting the burden of anticipated losses to others rather than by preventing the possibility of the loss. The economic and legal vehicle for risk shifting is known as insurance. Insurance is a contract whereby a third party agrees to compensate the subscriber for specified costs incurred when a specified loss occurs.

The price of an insurance contract has various components. The primary component is the expected loss, which is simply the total loss insured against multiplied by the probability that the loss will occur. A $1 million life insurance policy for a person whose chance of dying during the policy's term is 1 percent has an expected loss of $10,000. The second component, referred to from the subscriber's perspective as the "risk premium," is the amount beyond the expected loss that the subscriber is willing to pay to avoid bearing the full brunt of the loss. If the life insurance policy just described is purchased at the total price of $11,000, it is worth $1,000 to policyholders to have the insurer assume the financial risk of their death. Subscribers would rather pay this "extra" $1,000 than either bear the risk of leaving their families without support or incur the cost of saving the $1 million themselves. For the insurer, the $1,000 covers the administrative costs of selling and servicing the contract, it provides a margin of profit, and it compensates the insurer for bearing the risk of having to make the payout.

Insurance not only shifts risk to the insurer but also has the salutary effect of reducing risk in the aggregate. This critical point in the economics of insurance is seldom appreciated by the public. Some people suppose that markets for insurance arise either because the insurance company knows more than the subscriber about the actual expected loss or the insurance company does not dislike risk as much as the subscriber does. Both suppositions are often far from true. Most subscribers know more, and often far more, than the insurer about their own risks. If insurers somehow did know more, a competitive insurance market would squeeze out most of the bargaining advantage to be gained from this superior knowledge. Second, most insurers are more risk averse than most consumers, even the famous Lloyds of London.

The actual economic reason that insurance is a welfare-enhancing transaction is that the pooling of risk decreases risk to a measurable and often dramatic extent. Insurance reduces risk even though it does not reduce (and, indeed, may increase) the probability of loss. This marvel of insurance requires additional explanation, using economic theory.

The concept of risk can be made more precise by distinguishing between the calculated odds that a bad event will occur, which is the primary risk, and the chance that the calculation might prove wrong as real events occur, which is the secondary risk. Secondary risk is an elusive concept that cannot readily be understood without some knowledge of mathematics and statistics, but the gist of it can be captured by an illustration. When flipping a coin, we know with nearly absolute certainty (partly from mathematical theory and partly from physical science) that the coin has a fifty-fifty chance of landing heads or tails. In any 100 actual flips, however, we may get 60/40 or 51/49 or sometimes exactly 50/50, but both statistics and actual experience tell us that we will not always get 50/50. This failure of the odds always to play out is known in statistics as variance. It is also the concept of secondary risk.

The core social benefit of insurance is that it reduces secondary risk by reducing variance. This reduction occurs through what is known as the law of large numbers, which states that, for a given risk (say, of a coin turning up tails), variance is reduced the more times the risk is incurred. The law can be verified by doing a 10-flip coin toss 1,000 times in a row, then doing a 1,000-flip coin toss 10 times in a row, and seeing in which 10,000-flip series the heads and tails most consistently come out 50/50. Intuition and computer simulation tell us that it will be the latter by a long shot.

Insurance reduces secondary risk, which is the risk that the calculated odds will not bear themselves out, by pooling a large number of similar risks. If 10,000 persons each face a 1 in 10,000 risk of dying from natural causes, which to each of them would impose a $1 million loss in financial security for their families, they face individually a tremendous amount of risk. If each simply contributes $100 to a pool that will pay out $1 million to anyone who dies from natural causes, they can be fairly certain that the pool will have to make only one $1 million payment. By this simple act of pooling, these 10,000 persons have reduced their individual risks to almost nothing, and they have created only a small risk for the pool. In short, risk has not merely been shifted or spread, it has been reduced in the aggregate.

If a separate company forms the pool (assume that it is non-profit), it will require a little extra—say $1,000—to cover administrative costs and to bear its own risk of having to make more than a single payout or to purchase its own insurance against that possibility. This extra amount divided 10,000 ways is only 10 cents each, far less than the maximum risk premium that each participant would likely be willing to pay beyond the primary risk of $100 for protection against such a catastrophic loss. Because there are enormous economies of scale both in the administrative costs of running the pool and in the benefits of secondary risk reduction that come from creating the pool, a risk becomes more easily insurable the larger the pool for a particular risk.

Why Not Insurance?

Now that we understand why some risks are insurable, we must explore why many, indeed most, risks are uninsurable to a significant extent. Risks become uninsurable when the economies and welfare enhancement created by shifting and pooling risks are insufficient to compensate for the administrative, capital, and risk aversion costs of accepting them. Then the market for formal insurance to cover the risk fails to develop or develops to a more limited extent than it might. The economic forces that affect insurability can be grouped into supply-side and demand-side factors.

On the supply side, the premium required to induce insurers to accept risk increases steadily as the size of the risk pool decreases. Many risk pools are too small to produce a sufficient risk reduction to offset the transaction costs of administration. If only 10 persons face a 1-in-10,000 risk of dying, for example, no company would promise to cover a $1 million loss for just $1,000 (10 times $100), even though the company faces only a 1-in-1,000 chance of having to make a payout. How much extra risk premium beyond the calculated loss of $1,000 would an insurer require to bear a 1-in-1,000 risk of having to pay out $1 million? It might be as much as $10,000. If so, the participants in a 10-member pool would have to pay $100 plus $1,000 rather than the $100 plus ten cents we assumed for a 10,000 member pool. In other words, a 1,000-fold decrease in the size of the pool might (this is pure speculation) produce a 10,000-fold increase in the per capita cost of the secondary risk.

Although these are hypothetical numbers, they are borne out to some extent by measured results in the health care market. Figure 2–1 shows the profit that remains from the premium paid by different sized employer groups, after all claims and administrative expenses are accounted for. This market-driven profit margin reflects in part the varying risk premium that insurers demand in order to insure different sized groups. The increased secondary risk that comes from a smaller risk pool requires insurers to charge small groups significantly more than large groups for the same coverage, even

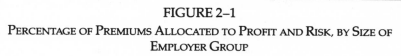

FIGURE 2–1

PERCENTAGE OF PREMIUMS ALLOCATED TO PROFIT AND RISK, BY SIZE OF
EMPLOYER GROUP

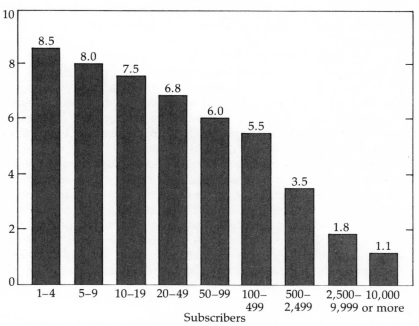

SOURCE: Congressional Research Service, 1990.

apart from administrative expenses entailed in selling and servicing the insurance contract. These increased costs naturally lessen the willingness of subscribers to buy.

The willingness to buy insurance is a demand-side factor that requires further explanation. The extent to which people dislike risk depends on the nature, magnitude, and degree of risk. We simply do not worry about some risks, either because they are not perceived as "risks" (for example, some people enjoy hang gliding *because* it is risky) or the harm is not that serious. It has been shown by experiment, for instance, that people are less willing to pay others to bear a risk that is either very likely (because the cost of insurance is almost as much as the loss itself) or that is very unlikely (because it is too remote to worry about). Flood insurance in a flood plain and flood insurance on a hill top are two examples. People are also more concerned about large, catastrophic losses than ones they can easily

9

absorb within ordinary earnings and savings.

Another way to capture the desirability of insurance is to distinguish between predictable and unpredictable losses. If we know that we will incur a moderate loss at the end of the year—say, having to buy Christmas presents—it makes great sense to set aside money in advance to bear the cost but not to pay someone else a premium to bear this risk. The same holds true even if the expected loss is very large. Pooling risks of virtual certainty does not reduce secondary risk because losses with virtual certainty have no secondary risk. Without significant reduction in secondary risk, an insurer would be unlikely to accept the risk for any price that a well-informed subscriber would be willing to pay. Only when individually unpredictable losses are made predictable in the aggregate by the mere act of pooling do desirable insurance products come into being.[2]

A distinction should also be made between insurance as a financing mechanism and insurance as a mechanism to reduce risk through risk pooling. A prepayment method for highly probable losses might be called insurance, but it is really only a financing mechanism with attendant transaction costs. Consider, for instance, an individual retirement account. A pension fund might be called a form of insurance against the costs of retirement, but it is really only a form of savings—of setting aside money for future use. We expect to make, not lose, money from savings, so we would not pay someone more to save our money than the investment is earning. Similarly, we have little to gain and much to lose from casting our savings into an undifferentiated risk pool with many others. The easier it is to protect against a financial risk through our own savings, the less insurable it is. Savings are a form of advance financing that should not be confused with insurance, any more than purchasing homeowner's insurance should be confused with paying a mortgage.

The size and predictability of risk are demand-side factors affecting the willingness to pay a risk premium. On the supply side of insurability, two other economic and behavioral phenomena affect the ability to structure efficient and stable risk pools. The first is known as adverse selection and the second as moral hazard.

---

2. This highlights the irony that, in the world of insurance, private markets work best when there is the least amount of information about individual risk, contrary to the ordinary rule that consumer ignorance causes market failure. A better way of stating the point is that insurance markets come into existence as a means to reduce the welfare loss created by uncertain risk; hence, the welfare gain from insurance is the least where the least uncertainty exists.

Adverse selection, also known as biased selection, occurs when potential subscribers know more about their individual risks than the insurer does, a condition economists call information asymmetry. Suppose, for instance, that a health insurer assumes that all persons of the same age and sex have the same risk of disease or injury and so prices its product accordingly—say, at $3,000 for males aged forty to forty-five. Naturally, not all persons of this age have the same risk of illness. Some are in excellent shape, some have average health, and some are sick. A disproportionate number of unhealthy people are likely to subscribe, because they will find the average price more attractive than those of lesser risk will. A pool of unhealthier-than-average subscribers will obviously end up costing more than $3,000 per person, so the insurer will raise its price—say to $3,500—to remain solvent. This does not solve the adverse selection problem, however, since even at this or any other above-average price, the insurance is more attractive to high-risk than to low-risk subscribers.

Adverse selection exists as an imperfection to some degree in any insurance market, even if it does not destroy the market. The market might find a stable equilibrium if there is a price that balances a few high-risk subscribers with many slightly-below-average ones. Nevertheless, adverse selection discourages at the margin the purchase of insurance by some lower-risk people who would otherwise have chosen to purchase it. At the extreme, adverse selection may destroy the market altogether since it tends to force a price that covers the highest group of risks, which as a consequence may be unaffordable for anyone.

One remedy for adverse selection is for insurers to ferret out information about the individual subscribers and to group and price them according to their actual risks. This is called risk selection (or risk assessment) and risk rating. More generically, this process is referred to as underwriting. The effect is to create multiple, separately priced risk pools that are each stable (that is, not subject to a price spiral). In life and health insurance, risk selection is done through questionnaires and medical examinations. In auto and home insurance, risk selection is done by examining driving records and neighborhood statistics for fire and theft. Ferreting out more refined risk information can be costly, however, and so the process can never be perfected. Insurers must strike a balance between the expense of risk assessment and the incremental advantage in offering a marketable product.

The other technique for solving adverse selection is to structure the insurance product in a manner that precludes individual selection according to subscribers' perceptions of their own risk. If insurance is sold to a group formed for reasons other than the purchase of insurance (such as employment or trade association), only the group's average risk, not each individual member's risk, need be assessed. For larger groups, risk rating can be done simply by examining the group's past experience, since losses for large groups, following the law of large numbers, are unlikely to differ markedly in the future from the past. Group risk suffices for groups formed for noninsurance reasons because it can be predicted that new members of the group will not be higher-than-average risks and that those who leave will not be lower-than-average risks. In other words, members will not select in or select out of the group just because of the insurance.

This happy solution of group insurance is not always available. If group members have a choice, the healthier ones will opt out and purchase individually at a rate cheaper than the average cost for the entire group. The group solution to adverse selection has worked in health insurance only because various tax laws and labor market conditions encourage employers to purchase it on behalf of their employees, which removes the element of choice within the group. Employer groups are convenient vehicles for this insurance, not only because of the economies of bulk purchase, but also because workers are healthier on average than nonworkers, and because people usually do not enter or leave the work force primarily for insurance.

Another threat to a successful insurance market is the tendency of insurance to increase the risk that is insured against—a phenomenon called moral hazard. Other things being equal, insured buildings are more likely to burn down than uninsured ones.[3] Although arson may be one reason, another is that the owners of insured buildings, consciously or not, may take fewer precautions against fire. Having purchased comprehensive insurance for a warehouse, why bother to install sprinklers or hire round-the-clock guards?

If moral hazard cannot be controlled, it can lead to overpricing of insurance and ultimately to the destruction of an insurance market. Who wants to buy insurance if doing so increases the risk? Even though this increased risk is shifted to the insurer, the additional cost it creates may shrink the risk pool to an uneconomical size.

Much of the structure and content of an insurance policy can be explained by the need to control moral hazard. The nature of the risk

---

3. The simple correlation noted does not establish that causation runs in this direction. Causation in the other direction, however, such as owners of fire-prone buildings deciding to buy more insurance, is an instance of the other market imperfection: adverse selection.

and the level of payout are defined in a manner to foreclose voluntary hazard creation or discretionary increases in the size of the loss. Thus, in life insurance, death is not easily faked and is not likely to be prompted by insurance (except for suicide, which is therefore not covered), provided that the insurance is held by the person whose life is insured or by someone who cares about that person. The concern expressed in this proviso is why the law forbids the purchase of life insurance by someone with only a casual interest in the person whose life is insured. Furthermore, to avoid litigation over how much support the deceased's dependents require, the payout is defined as a lump sum rather than as some amorphous concept of suffering or dependency.

In situations less catastrophic than death, moral hazard is controlled by requiring the subscriber to bear some portion of the cost in the event of loss. Health insurance does this through deductibles and copayments. Insurance that is frequently renewed, like auto, home, or health insurance, deters moral hazard by basing the insurance on the subscriber's loss experience. As with adverse selection, however, moral hazard can never be eliminated entirely, and any attempt to minimize it carries a cost. It can be an explicit cost, such as the price of monitoring for abuse, or implicit, such as reducing the scope of benefits.

Whither Health Insurance?

Considering all of the obstacles to the insurability of risks, one might wonder why health insurance ever flourished, not just why it is now withering on the vine. Indeed, in the early part of the twentieth century, health care was thought to be uninsurable. Life insurance companies would not venture into health care because, as compared with the risk of death, the risk of incurring medical expenses was thought to be insufficiently severe and too subject to the market-destroying effects of adverse selection and moral hazard. At the beginning of the twentieth century, medicine was low-tech, ineffective, and only modestly expensive. Feverish brows were mopped, herbal remedies were administered, and surgery was near-barbaric. Health care was not so essential as it is today and not so expensive as to threaten catastrophic loss.

On the supply side, insurers could not envision an economical solution to the adverse selection problems that spring from widely varying health status. Even more difficult were the moral hazard problems of defining what benefits are due a sick person. The risk is not that insurance will induce poor health habits, for it insures not against poor health but against the cost of medical care. Insurers could foresee the difficulties in defining how much medical care is due as a result of a particular illness in comparison with, for instance, house repair costs after a storm.

In the 1930s, Blue Cross became the first to overcome these obstacles when it marketed a successful hospital insurance policy. By that time, hospitalization was seen as essential for surgery to correct a number of life-threatening or disabling conditions (such as appendicitis and hernia repair) as well as for childbirth. Moral hazard problems were controlled by charging deductibles and copayments and by limiting the benefits to a specified number of days or a total amount of reimbursement. Adverse selection, however, was more of a problem.

As is now well known, Blue Cross began pricing its policies on a strict community-rated basis without regard to age or health status, but it soon had to modify or abandon this practice in most locations because of competition from commercial insurers.[4] When Blue Cross was the only health insurer, the problems of adverse selection were not so severe as to cripple the market. Even though insisting on one price for everyone might have deterred some people from buying, Blue Cross did not lose business to competing insurers. Only when commercial life insurers saw Blue Cross's success and so entered the market did adverse selection problems become manifest. Commercial insurers began to underprice Blue Cross by selling to younger, healthier subscribers, leaving Blue Cross with an older, more infirm population.

Still, adverse selection was partially solved through employer-based group insurance. After World War II, two strong but artificial incentives induced employers to offer health insurance to their workers. The first was the exemption of fringe benefits from the postwar wage and price controls. Freezing cash wages forced employers to compete in the labor market by enhancing fringe benefits. Second, the exclusion of fringe benefits from personal income taxes led employees to accept lower wages in exchange for enhanced benefits. Instead of the employees purchasing health insurance for themselves from their after-tax income, employers purchased it for them from

---

4. For recent accounts, see Field and Shapiro, *Employment and Health Benefits*, pp. 51–85; John K. Iglehart, "The American Health Care System: Private Insurance," *New England Journal of Medicine*, vol. 326 (1992), pp. 1715–20; Randall R. Bovbjerg, Charles C. Griffin, and Caitlin Carroll, "U.S. Health Care Coverage and Costs: Historical Development and Choices for the 1990s," *Journal of Law, Medicine and Ethics*, vol. 21, no. 2 (1993), pp. 141–62.

their before-tax income. The marginal tax rate determined the size of the implicit subsidy that the government provided for the cost of the insurance.[5]

Employers' willingness to purchase health insurance for their employees as a group allowed the health insurance market to flourish. The main factor was not, as is often thought, that employees as a whole are healthier than the nonworkers; unhealthy groups might have been just as willing or even more willing to purchase. Rather, it was that employer group sales structured the market in a way that resolved the major adverse selection problems. As discussed above, insurers selling to groups formed for noninsurance reasons need not worry that they are being selected against within the group, that is, that unhealthy persons are joining in disproportionate numbers or that healthy persons are leaving disproportionately. Moreover, because a group purchases in bulk for all its members, insurers could assess the group risk by observing its recent claims experience rather than by having to measure and sum each individual's risk. These structural features and the legal inducements mentioned above allowed employer-sponsored health insurance to grow rapidly during the 1950s and become widespread by the 1960s.

Other portions of the health insurance market fared less well. Left out were the poor, who cannot afford insurance, and the elderly and disabled, who do not have jobs and for whom insurance is very expensive. The deterioration of Blue Cross's communitywide rating practices made it necessary for the government to enact social insurance programs for these two groups in the form of Medicaid and Medicare.

The combination of private insurance for workers and social insurance for the poor, disabled, and elderly proved to be a stable and widely applauded social compromise for a decade or so. Private markets were allowed to operate without extensive oversight where they functioned well, and social programs picked up most of those not covered by private markets. Now this compromise is in serious jeopardy because the territory traditionally covered by private insurance is quickly shrinking in a manner that is difficult for social entitlement programs to absorb. This is why reform is being driven much more by the emerging defects in the private market than by the funding woes of the government programs. Of the 37 million people

---

5. According to calculations made by Lewin/VHI, in 1991 this tax subsidy resulted in forgoing $66.6 billion in federal taxes and $8.3 billion in state taxes. Uwe E. Reinhardt, "Reorganizing the Financial Flows in American Health Care," *Health Affairs*, vol. 12, supp. (1993), p. 180.

who are uninsured, about 85 percent live in families headed by a person who works some time during the year, and more than half of the uninsured are full-time, full-year workers or their family members.[6]

The Disintegration of Health Insurance

The fairly stable compromise between social and private insurance has begun to fail because the risk pools centered on private employers began to unravel. These problems developed in three phases, beginning with individual subscribers, proceeding to small employee groups of twenty-five or less, and now reaching larger groups of up to a hundred.

Individual Insurance. Problems in the health insurance market appeared first among individual subscribers—people such as independent contractors, free lance artists, and others who are self-employed and so must seek out health insurance on their own. This part of the market has always been plagued by adverse selection. Younger, healthier individuals often decline to purchase insurance until they anticipate significant expenses, for the birth of a child, for example, or for the onset of a chronic disease. Those who purchase individually therefore tend to be significantly more risky than those insured through employer groups. And, because employers demand that their groups be rated according to their particular claims history, an insurer cannot include in its pool for individual subscribers the broad base of healthier subscribers in its employer groups. The insurer then has to raise the price to a level that many individuals cannot afford or are not willing to pay unless they know they are likely to use the benefits.

As a consequence, insurers have been forced to adopt a set of practices, known generically as medical underwriting, that limit the availability of individual insurance. First, they rate applicants according to their individual age and health status, pricing the insurance out of the reach of older or chronically ill people. Second, to discourage subscribers from enrolling only when they are ill, insurers impose preexisting illness provisions that, for instance, will not cover for one to two years conditions that existed any time during the six to twelve months before enrollment. These provisions make individual insurance much less attractive to unhealthy patients. Still,

---

6. Employee Benefit Research Institute analysis of the March 1991 Current Population Survey.

16

many would choose to pay the premiums for a year or more to be covered thereafter, since most states make it difficult for insurers not to renew health insurance. Therefore, insurers refuse entirely to cover individuals of particularly high risk or they exclude altogether designated health problems (such as cancer or diabetes).

To screen for individual health risk, insurers engage in an intensive risk-assessment process. Detailed questionnaires on health status are administered, thorough medical examinations are given, and a centralized database of information shared among insurers (known as the Medical Information Bureau) is consulted to determine whether the applicant has been turned down by another insurer or has been quoted an increased rate, and for what reasons.[7]

Refusing insurance, increasing premiums, and limiting coverage have been common business practices in the individual health insurance market for decades, even by some Blue Cross plans. These forms of medical underwriting were tolerated until recently because they were confined to a narrow part of the private insurance market. The worst excesses of medical underwriting can be handled through several means. Fourteen states require Blue Cross to offer community-rated insurance on an open-enrollment basis. Blue Cross's ability to negotiate with providers for discounts, as well as the tax exemption it enjoys in most states, helps to keep its insurance affordable. A couple of dozen other states have created high-risk pools for individuals who are denied coverage or quoted substandard rates. These pools are partially subsidized by a premium tax on the insurance industry or by general tax revenues. As a final safety net, those without coverage can "spend down" their assets and income to qualify for Medicaid.

Small-Group Health Insurance. For a time, this patchwork system, while far from ideal, sufficed to avoid abandoning or reconstituting the entire insurance market. Recent years have witnessed a much greater sense of crisis about private insurance, however. Primarily, this change occurred because the practices previously reserved to individual insurance are being applied to small and medium-sized employer groups.

As explained above, risk rating of larger employer groups is accomplished by observing the group's recent claims history. This practice allows a form of community rating to be used, one that sets a single rate for each employment group as a community. As employee groups decrease in size, the ability to predict a group's future ex-

7. See note 8 below.

penses from its past claims diminishes. Therefore, insurers tradition-ally applied a modified form of community rating to all their small groups as a block. They would price their policies according to the average claims experience for all their small-group business, adjusting only for the age of individual enrollees. Age-adjusted community rating proved to be a workable rating practice for many years.

The recent breakdown in private insurance has occurred primar-ily because small-employer groups are being subjected to the same risk selection and medical underwriting techniques that are applied to individual insurance subscribers. This trend has resulted from several related forces, all driven by the rapidly increasing costs of health care.

First, the cost of health care has pushed up the price of health insurance at such a rapid rate that not all small employers can afford it. Small employers are frequently start-up companies with tenuous profit margins and heavy debt expenses. Established small employers often are small for a reason—they have been less than successful. Many low-wage jobs are concentrated in small firms.

If there is significant unemployment, small employers can cut fringe benefit costs and still attract a sufficient work force. Even without significant unemployment, small employers can save labor costs by offering a wage-benefit package that is lean on benefits but still attractive to healthier workers.

This natural sorting of the labor market would ordinarily be considered an efficient matching of resources and preferences, but it creates problems by drawing off healthier workers from the commu-nity of insured small-group workers. This bleeding off of healthier workers sets into motion a classic adverse selection spiral. Since the remaining pool is less healthy on average than before, the rates go up even more than the underlying trend in health care costs (which are high in themselves). These increases force more small employers with healthier workers to drop out of the risk pool, while those who remain shop more aggressively over price.

In response, insurers have been forced to break apart the commu-nity-rated small-group risk pool by offering risk-rated premiums to healthier groups.[8] Although Blue Cross and large commercial insur-

---

8. The following summary account is taken from a number of sources, including Wendy K. Zellers, Catherine G. McLaughlin, and Kevin D. Frick, "Small-Business Health Insurance: Only the Healthy Need Apply," *Health Affairs*, vol. 11, no. 1 (Spring 1992), pp. 174–80; Catherine G. McLaughlin, "The Dilemma of Affordability—Health Insurance for Small Businesses," in Robert B. Helms, ed., *American Health Policy: Critical Issues for Reform* (Washington, D.C.: AEI Press, 1993), pp. 152–66; Deborah Stone, "The Struggle for the Soul of Health Insurance," *Journal of Health Politics, Policy and*

ers initially resisted these trends, smaller upstart insurers looking for a profitable market niche soon forced most dominant companies to follow suit. Risk rating requires insurers to use the same forms of risk assessment that are applied to individual subscribers—questionnaires and medical examinations—which adds to administrative expenses. As a result of medical underwriting, some subscribers are turned down outright or priced at a level they cannot afford. Finally, to fight the effects of adverse selection, insurers have imposed lengthy exclusions for preexisting conditions or other broad exclusions from coverage. Preexisting-condition exclusions are a particular problem in this market given the high job turnover rate and the large number of seasonal and temporary employees among small employers.

In some ways, the medical underwriting techniques used in the small-group market have become even worse for subscribers and for the market than those traditionally used for individual subscribers. The large number of small employers allows some smaller insurance companies to stay in business selecting only good risks. These insurers, known as cherry pickers or cream skimmers for their willingness to take only the safest risks, adopt overinclusive techniques for risk selection. One is rating by industry, whereby insurers refuse to cover a growing number of blacklisted professions or occupations, such as manufacturers and miners, who are likely to include workers with poorer health, or lawyers and doctors, who are likely to be more demanding in seeking medical care. These categorical distinctions resemble the socially offensive practice of redlining by geographic area that is prohibited in life, homeowner's, and other lines of insurance.

Other disturbing underwriting practices have evolved. One, known euphemistically as postclaims underwriting, is to issue insurance freely but with lengthy preexisting exclusion clauses that are aggressively applied when claims are presented. This practice allows insurers to avoid evaluating the health status of applicants unless they end up submitting costly claims. This behavior is regulated with two-year "incontestability clauses" in life and other forms of insurance, but not in health insurance, which is issued or renewed annually or semiannually.

A second problem created by preexisting exclusion clauses is

Law, vol. 18, no. 2 (Summer 1993), pp. 286–317; U.S. General Accounting Office, "Employer-based Health Insurance: High Costs, Wide Variation Threaten System," September 1992; U.S. Congress, Office of Technology Assessment, "Genetic Tests and Health Insurance: Results of a Survey" (Washington, D.C.: Government Printing Office, October 1992).

that employees who have outlasted them may be reluctant to start again with another insurer. Chronically ill employees, or those with sick family members, may be frozen into their present position by the fear of losing benefits for one to two years if they switch to another insurer. According to one account, up to one quarter of American workers may be affected by this condition of "job-lock."[9]

Small-group insurers have also been accused of "churning." This is the practice of offering deep discounts to new subscribers based on their initial good health profiles and then imposing price increases of 50 to 100 percent or more after a year or two of coverage, or refusing to renew altogether. Frequently, these price increases and refusals to serve an entire small group are based not on actual adverse claims history of the group but on the "wearing off" of the predictive power of the initial screening. Medical underwriting tends to wear off by virtue of the statistical phenomenon of regression to the mean, according to which unusually good risks tend over time to become normal risks simply by the operation of the law of averages. Prices also rise over time simply because the initial preexisting condition periods expire, typically after a year or two.

These abusive practices should not indict all forms of medical underwriting. Some degree of risk adjustment is acceptable and perhaps desirable. Without underwriting, individuals would wait until they were sick before purchasing health insurance, which would be like buying fire insurance for a burning house. As a consequence of this adverse selection, insurance would become so expensive that no one could afford it, and the market might collapse entirely. Some incentive is needed to induce the early purchase of insurance while subscribers are still healthy. Nevertheless, the techniques for underwriting have become so numerous and aggressive that they are destroying rather than stabilizing the market. Only those who need health insurance least can afford it—and when their health status changes, coverage is often dropped or restricted. This is reflected in the Lewin/ICF finding (in "The Relationship between Firm Size and the Health Care Cost of Workers," 1994) that, on average, the health care costs of insured groups under twenty-five is one-quarter less than the costs of larger groups. In short, the individual and small group market is tending to produce a form of pseudo-insurance that offers little protection when it is really needed.

The consequence for coverage in the small-group market has been disastrous. The core of employers unwilling or unable to afford

9. P. Taylor, "Tying Choices to Health Coverage," *Washington Post*, January 26, 1992.

FIGURE 2–2

PERCENTAGE OF EMPLOYERS THAT OFFER HEALTH INSURANCE, BY SIZE, 1991

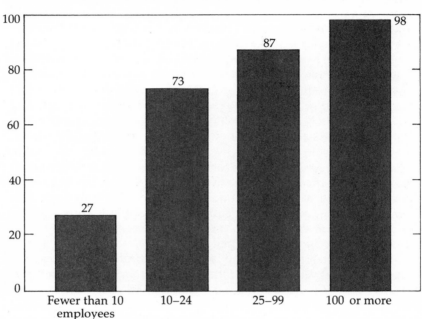

SOURCE: Cynthia B. Sullivan, Marianne Miller, and Claudia C. Johnson, *Employer-Sponsored Health Insurance in 1991* (Washington, D.C.: Health Insurance Association of America, 1992).

insurance has increased because of the underlying costs of health care. The number of employers with work forces whose age or health status prices insurance out of reach has also increased, since only one employee with an expensive illness like cancer or heart disease can make the costs for the rest of the group many times higher than average. Finally, even for groups of average good health, the overhead expense of selling and administering insurance on this smaller scale has driven up the price. By some estimates, overhead for small-group insurance can amount to as much as 40 percent of premiums, compared with 6 percent or less for the largest groups.[10] Even for groups of average-to-excellent health working for employers that are not in financial distress, this may be too high a risk premium

10. U.S. Congressional Research Service, "Private Health Insurance: Options for Reform" (Washington, D.C.: Government Printing Office, September 1990).

to pay. Employers may drop coverage altogether, or require their employees to pay an increasing portion of the premium—in some instances 50 percent or more even for single (nonfamily) coverage. Shifting more costs to employees causes more of the healthier ones to opt out of the insured group, further diminishing the risk pool.

About 40 percent of the total work force is employed by firms with fewer than twenty-five employees. These small employers account for about two-thirds of uninsured workers and their dependents, however, reflecting the far greater difficulty of insuring small groups.[11] Further reflecting this relationship between group size and market breakdown, the level of employee coverage is directly in proportion to the size of the work force (see figures 2–2 and 2–3).

Larger Groups. As health care costs have increased at double-digit rates each year, these difficulties have spread to ever larger groups. The higher price of insurance makes employers more selective in buying insurance, encouraging insurers to adopt ever more aggressive forms of medical underwriting. When these problems first appeared, they were mainly confined to groups of ten or fewer. A few years ago, the insurance industry focused its reform efforts on groups of up to twenty-five. More recently, legislation for insurance market reform has encompassed groups up to fifty, and evidence indicates that significant medical underwriting (and hence adverse selection) occurs at levels of a hundred or more.[12] Indeed, as figure 2–4 shows, the rate at which insurance is being dropped now appears much greater among groups of 25–100 employees than for smaller groups.

Paradoxically, the prevalence of insurance itself is partly responsible for the increase in health care costs. Health care costs have increased dramatically because of the moral hazard problems created by the form into which health insurance has evolved. Encouraged by unions and by tax policy, employers abandoned the attributes of health insurance intended to combat its tendency to increase the cost of treatment. Health insurance coverage was made more comprehensive, extending from hospitalization to outpatient treatment and prescription drugs. Dollar caps and service limits were removed,

---

11. Michael A. Morrisey, "Mandating Benefits and Compensating Differentials—Taxing the Uninsured," in Robert B. Helms, ed., *American Health Policy: Critical Issues for Reform* (Washington, D.C.: AEI Press, 1993), p. 135 (based on an Employee Benefits Research Institute report).

12. Stone, "Struggle for the Soul of Health Insurance," pp. 286–317; U.S. Congress, Office of Technology Assessment, "Genetic Tests and Health Insurance."

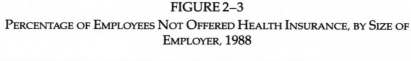

FIGURE 2–3

PERCENTAGE OF EMPLOYEES NOT OFFERED HEALTH INSURANCE, BY SIZE OF EMPLOYER, 1988

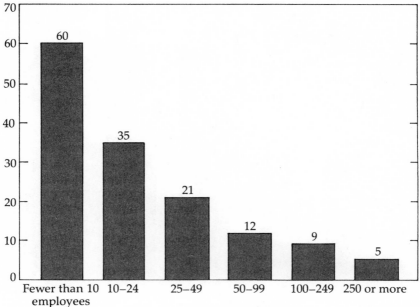

SOURCE: Stephen H. Long and M. Susan Marquis tabulation of May 1988 Current Population Survey.

and "first-dollar" coverage was created by lowering deductibles and coinsurance. Insurance was also extended into discretionary areas, such as mental health and long-term care, and to routine expenses such as dental and preventive care. And, throughout the history of health insurance, decisions on how to apply the basic criterion for coverage—medically necessary treatment—have been left primarily to the very physicians who are paid by the insurance proceeds.[13]

The moral hazard problems created by this liberalization of health insurance explain why it has been necessary to adopt managed-care techniques, such as utilization review, and to reinstate policy limitations, such as substantial deductibles and copayments. These moral hazard ills are not unique to private insurance: they

13. Mark A. Hall and Gerard F. Anderson, "Health Insurers' Assessment of Medical Technology," *University of Pennsylvania Law Review*, vol. 140 (1992), pp. 1637–1712.

FIGURE 2–4

PERCENTAGE OF EMPLOYERS OFFERING HEALTH INSURANCE, BY SIZE, 1989, 1990, AND 1991

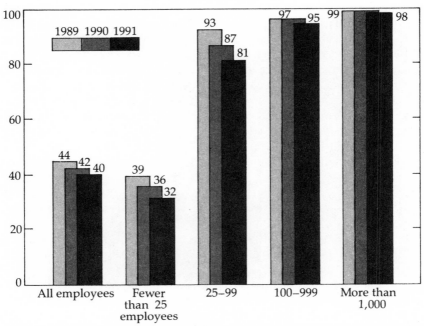

SOURCE: Health Insurance Association of America Employer Surveys, 1989, 1990, and 1991.

afflict the government programs just as seriously. Only the adverse selection problems are unique to private insurance, and they are compounded by the increasingly uninsurable nature of the comprehensive set of benefits.

Health care costs are becoming uninsurable by conventional insurance criteria even for large groups. Full-coverage health insurance is becoming less marketable, even in the portion of the market that functions best, because it covers risks that individuals can predict and are too small and routine to be worth paying a risk premium for. The difference between insurance as a risk pooling mechanism and insurance as a financing mechanism was explained earlier: insurance works best where pooling risk reduces uncertainty, which occurs only for losses that are unpredictable at an individual level. If subscribers know they are likely to see a doctor several times a year or to require prescription medication, dental care, or eyeglasses, they can

24

more easily and efficiently set money aside in a savings account than pay someone else to bear these costs. Expanding standard insurance to cover these costs makes the product less marketable.

Nevertheless, such insurance has continued to sell as a result of the implicit tax subsidy for employer-paid health expenses. Because of this subsidy, the costs of predictable health needs are less than what employees would have to pay from aftertax wages, despite the administrative costs of paying for the subsidized care through an insurance mechanism. Insuring discretionary expenditures creates an insoluble moral hazard problem, however, that is driving up the cost of health insurance to a level that makes it unattractive despite the tax subsidy. Some employers are trimming benefits or asking their employees to pay for more of the premium; others are dropping insurance altogether. An intermediate solution, which is beginning to be discussed but which is not yet widely implemented, is to establish "medical savings accounts" as a tax-preferred mechanism for employees to pay predictable medical expenses out-of-pocket; purchased health insurance can then be restricted to catastrophic expenses.

Another route for larger employers to minimize benefit costs is to self-insure. Health care costs become predictable and therefore not economically insurable for a much greater range of treatment at a collective level. For a large group of employees, even major expenses such as hospitalization and surgery are predictable based on recent experience. An employer has little reason to pay more than the expected loss if the uncertainty (secondary risk) has been greatly reduced by the decision to purchase on behalf of a large pool of employees. Such employers can more economically self-insure most of their employees and purchase insurance only at a stop-loss level for catastrophic (far-more-than-expected) losses.

The trend toward self-insurance is hastened by another kind of artificial stimulus, contained in the preemption provisions of the Employee Retirement Income Security Act of 1974 (ERISA). This federal act, designed to regulate pension and other employee welfare benefits, inadvertently overrides a wide body of state insurance regulation for self-insured employers without replacing it with federal oversight. Self-insured employers avoid paying premium taxes and are free to alter benefits at will. For these and other reasons, the great majority of large-employer groups are now partially or fully self-insured. The loss of large, profitable employer business to self-insurance reduces the market share of existing insurers and so intensifies the pressures to engage in medical underwriting.

In sum, we are witnessing the not-so-gradual unraveling of a workable private market, beginning at its smallest end of individual subscribers and very small-employer groups and progressing to medium-sized and larger firms. This relentless progression is driven by market forces (partially distorted as they are by the tax code and ERISA preemption), in response to the ever increasing costs of medical treatment—costs that are increasing in large part because of the comprehensiveness of health insurance. The task that faces state and federal lawmakers is to tie these frayed ends of the health insurance market back together at the same time that they create mechanisms to restrain health care costs. Before moving on to the specific reform proposals that help achieve this goal, we will take one additional detour into social and economic theory that will enhance our understanding of the problem and the most desirable solutions.

The Social Function of Health Insurance

Before attempting to restore order to the private health insurance market, we should inquire why the market system is worth fixing, rather than abandoning, and what social benefits come from a market system for pricing and delivering health insurance. Health care is too important for reform to be driven merely by a general reluctance to rely on governmental solutions.

Conventional Insurance. It is becoming commonplace to observe in health policy discussions that risk selection and segmentation contradict the traditional function of insurance, which is to spread risk as broadly as possible.[14] The preceding chapters help us understand why this is a distorted, if not incorrect, view of insurance generally. Insurance works best as insurance when it spreads risks broadly, but it also serves important social functions when it does not. There are many risks in life that it would be socially counterproductive to insure (such as the risk of failing an examination, or the risk of being found guilty of aggravated assault). To understand how this key point applies to health insurance, we should begin with more conventional lines of insurance.

---

14. For example, Stone, "The Struggle for the Soul of Health Insurance," pp. 286–317. See also Norman Daniels, "Insurability and the HIV Epidemic: Ethical Issues in Underwriting," *Milbank Quarterly*, vol. 68, no. 4 (1990), pp. 497–525; Robert A. Padgug and Gerald M. Oppenheimer, "AIDS, Health Insurance, and the Crisis of Community," *Notre Dame Journal of Law, Ethics and Public Policy*, vol. 5 (1990), pp. 35–51; Donald W. Light, "The Practice and Ethics of Risk-rated Health Insurance," *Journal of the American Medical Association*, vol. 267, no. 18 (1992), pp. 2503–8.

For conventional insurance covering fire, theft, death, or other losses, private markets serve to determine the optimal trade-off among risk bearing, risk reduction, and risk shifting.[15] The market's pricing mechanism signals to consumers the costs and benefits of their decisions. Specifically, the tendency of private markets to sort risks into homogenous groups helps to price each subscriber's risk as accurately as is feasible (given the costs of obtaining accurate risk information). Subscribers who receive accurate pricing signals can then decide which is preferable: to go without insurance and either bear the risk or invest in risk reduction; or to pay a risk premium for shifting and pooling the risk. Risk-rated insurance results in a better allocation of resources and in a better level of investment in risk prevention and risk spreading than would probably result from decisions made at a social level. Few Americans would want government to decide how much or how little they should save for dependents in lieu of life or disability insurance. Socializing all insurance would be tantamount to socializing the economy.

Private markets prevail for conventional insurance because the interests protected are such that it maximizes social welfare to allow individual preferences to vary widely. That some persons may choose to spend or not to spend their resources in a manner that others consider foolish is not reason enough to abandon private markets for conventional insurance. From society's perspective, individuals may choose to purchase fire or life insurance or not, and they may choose to install fire protective devices and set aside savings or not. Since these choices are determined by the same personal preferences that determine other consumptive decisions, the government would be thought overly intrusive to dictate that everyone maintain a certain level of insurance for home or life. The government's role is restricted to supplying minimal subsistence and shelter for those who are left destitute, whether by life's misfortunes or by their own or their provider's improvidence.

Health Insurance. To sum up, for conventional insurance, private markets produce two social goods: they help to determine the socially optimal level of insurance and they assist in making the best allocation of resources between insurance and risk reduction. Both of these social benefits contemplate a fair number of people not insuring at all or insuring far less than others. This point highlights the essential difference in the social function of health insurance.

---

15. Kenneth Abraham, *Distributing Risk: Insurance, Legal Theory, and Public Policy* (New Haven: Yale University Press, 1986).

More than for any other form of insurance, we rely on health insurance to supply a basic social need. Insurance is not relevant at all to food, clothing, and education, and it is relevant to housing only at the margin. In American health care, however, insurance is at the center. Unlike the socialized delivery of care in Great Britain and other countries, our system depends on insurance because doctors and hospitals are in the private sector (except for limited arenas such as state and municipal hospitals, the Department of Veterans Affairs, and the Indian Health Service). Because health care providers are private, and because the costs of care are so high, insurance in some form—either public or private—is essential for adequate access.

Some defenders of the status quo in the private health insurance market say that access to health care should not be equated with access to health insurance, since the government has other means to fulfill the social responsibility of minimally decent care for all. In the reality in which we live, however, this would be an invitation to socialization of medical practice, which defenders of the status quo hardly find appealing.

Aware of these social realities, the health insurance industry has struggled to find saving graces in a voluntary private market but so far has only made the anemic assertion that individual choice is a paramount value that government insurance would sacrifice. The choice to obtain no health insurance at all is not a socially valued preference. An individual's decision to go without health care imposes a social cost on others (what economists call an externality). Society's unwillingness to witness preventable death and suffering prompts us to save those who have no insurance, imposing greater costs on those of us who buy insurance. Nonpurchasers of insurance are free riders on the public's humanitarian spirit.

The value of pluralism must be articulated in some other way if it is to carry any weight in the social debate. The key insight is that variable preferences for health insurance do exist and are socially relevant when exercised above a minimal level. Assuming that a social minimum can be set and enforced, private market defenders argue that individuals should be able to choose whether or not to pay for first-dollar care and for discretionary areas of coverage. They should also be allowed to select insurance that determines where medical care will be delivered and the medical standards physicians will follow. Allowing preferences to vary in this way satisfies the economist's criterion of allocative efficiency and enhances social welfare. The principal attack comes from the egalitarian camp—those who place greater weight on equity among social classes and so would enforce uniform health insurance benefits and uniform quality of care.

Rather than defend market advocates against the egalitarian critique, I will assume that private insurance will be retained. Therefore, I will articulate the strongest rationale for its existence. Knowing what social benefits it offers, we can seek to maximize those benefits as we undertake its rehabilitation. We learn from this analysis that private health insurance is put to best use if a social minimum is enforced and if purchasing decisions are allowed to vary above that minimum as widely as is feasible (given practical concerns of administrability). Concerns about equity should address how high to set the social minimum or whether we should have a private system at all. But to rely on a private system without allowing some room for consumer preferences would be to abandon one of the central values of the system.

The second social benefit created by private markets is the role they play in influencing the level of risk reduction. The difficulty in extrapolating from conventional lines of insurance is that health risks appear less controllable than fire, theft, or other risks. Therefore, the pricing mechanism may not supply useful signals about risk reduction behavior. How my insurance is priced will not alter my genetic make-up or enable me individually to control environmental hazards.

Whether risk-rated insurance will encourage healthier habits (such as exercising, eating right, and not smoking) is a matter of considerable controversy, with little empirical evidence. Some argue that such habits are formed or broken regardless of the costs of insurance or treatment. If the threat of a debilitating illness or painful death is not sufficient to persuade someone to break the habit, a few extra dollars each month for insurance premiums probably will not matter.[16] Human psychology is not so one-dimensional, however, as to be reducible to such simplistic extrapolations. Modest financial incentives might have a stronger effect than the risk of death because money is an immediate reward and death is subject to psychological denial. In fact, several studies have demonstrated a strong association between increased costs and improved health habits.[17]

---

16. For a strong expression of this view, see Robert L. Schwartz, "Making Patients Pay for Their Life-Style Choices," *Cambridge Quarterly of Healthcare Ethics*, vol. 4 (1992), pp. 393–400.

17. Cigarette smoking, for example, has been shown to have a price elasticity of demand of about −.5, which means that a 10 percent increase in the costs of cigarettes produces about a 5 percent reduction in smoking. Theodore E. Keeler, Teh-Wei Hu, Paul G. Barnett, and Willard G. Manning, "Taxation, Regulation, and Addiction: A Demand Function for Cigarettes Based on Time-Series Evidence," *Journal of Health Economics*, vol. 12 (1993),

Even if *individuals* do not respond strongly to risk-rated insurance, *employers* certainly do, and it is employers that have the largest stake in the cost of insurance. Mainly because group insurance is now experience rated, many employers are instituting health promotion and wellness programs that are capable of having a major beneficial influence on employees' health. These programs include on-site exercise facilities, flu shots, and cancer screening. They also include targeted financial incentives to quit smoking, lose weight, improve diets, and the like. Most evaluations of these programs show them to be highly effective.[18] Experience-rated workers' compensation insurance has been shown to have the same positive influence on employers' workplace safety efforts.[19]

Risk-rating has efficiency advantages even if it is has no effect on actual health because it creates incentives to control the costs of health care. Health insurance does not insure against bad health any more than life insurance protects one from death. The risk protected is the cost of treatment, which is controllable to some degree. If subscribers' decisions about whether and where to seek treatment, and about the kind and extent of treatment, are at all discretionary, market incentives may play an important role in reducing the cost of health insurance. The same point can be made from the supply side. Even if subscribers' decisions on treatment are not influenced by

---

pp. 1–18. One corporation that required its workers to pay $250 a year more for each of four specified risk factors (overweight, high cholesterol, high blood pressure, and smoking) saw health insurance claims for participants decline by 42 percent, while claims for nonparticipants rose 92 percent, and the program also helped the employees lose weight, lower their blood pressure, and quit smoking. *BNA Health Care Daily*, July 8, 1993.

18. James Fries et al., "Reducing Health Care Costs by Reducing the Need and Demand for Medical Services," *New England Journal of Medicine*, vol. 329 (1993), pp. 321–25; Regina E. Herzlinger and David Calkins, "How Companies Tackle Health Care Costs: Part III," *Harvard Business Review* (January–February 1986), pp. 70–79.

19. Christopher J. Bruce and Frank J. Atkins, "Efficiency Effects of Premium-setting Regimes under Worker's Compensation: Canada and the United States," *Journal of Labor Economics*, vol. 11 (1993), pp. S38–S67 (a change from community to experience rating reduced the fatality rate by 40 percent in forestry and 20 percent in construction); M. Moore and W. K. Viscusi, *Compensation Mechanisms for Job Risks: Wages, Workers' Compensation, and Product Liability* (Princeton: Princeton University Press, 1990) (workers' compensation in general reduces fatality rates 27 percent); John W. Ruser, "Workers' Compensation Insurance, Experience-Rating, and Occupational Injuries," *RAND Journal of Economics*, vol. 16 (1985), pp. 487–503.

insurance costs, their insurance-purchasing decisions certainly are.[20] Private insurers therefore have a profit incentive to hold down the costs of treatment as long as the quality of the insurance product is not compromised excessively. For either cost-reduction mechanism to work, however, insurers must be allowed to vary the price of insurance. Otherwise, there will be no reward for economizing behavior.

Thus, if private markets are to serve their best social function, insurers must compete not on the basis of risk selection but on risk management. Risk selection has its strongest social purpose where insurance behaves in the classic manner of reducing uncertainty by pooling risks. This is one function, but not the central function, of health insurance, which has become more a prepayment financing mechanism than a true insurance mechanism—one that reduces risk by pooling. The pure insurance function of health insurance has diminished because it covers losses that are highly predictable by individual and group purchasers.

Health insurers serve their most useful social function by controlling the costs of treatment rather than by simply measuring and projecting those costs. Health insurance market reform seeks to harness the forces of competition to reduce the inappropriate costs of medical treatment and to preserve appropriate quality and spur medical advances. Accomplishing this objective requires that the energies previously applied to assessing individual health status (medical underwriting) be redirected to managing the treatment environment. Social objectives also require that health insurers price and offer their policies in a manner that does not undermine universal coverage. The remainder of this book will analyze how these goals can be accomplished, either under a system of voluntary health insurance purchase like that now in place or under a system of mandatory purchase like that proposed both by President Clinton and by Senate Republicans.

---

20. Michael Morrisey, *Price Sensitivity in Health Care: Implications for Health Care Policy* (Washington, D.C.: National Federation of Independent Business Foundation, 1992), pp. 108–24.

3
Insurance Market Reform under a System of Voluntary Purchase

Faced with possible extinction, the private health insurance industry has emerged as a vocal advocate of reforming the way it does business.

The Genesis of Market Reform Proposals

Since 1990, the following health insurance trade associations have proposed extensive regulation of the pricing, marketing, underwriting, and design of small-group health insurance: the Health Insurance Association of America (HIAA), which represents commercial insurers; the Blue Cross and Blue Shield Association (Blue Cross); the National Association of Insurance Commissioners (NAIC), which is composed of all state insurance regulators; and the Group Health Association of America (GHAA), which represents health maintenance organizations (HMOs). These reform initiatives are motivated by the insurance industry's desire to prevent the collapse of a private financing system. The industry is also concerned with avoiding simplistic corrections, such as pure community rating, that would threaten the viability of the market or of individual companies. The industry is proposing a more complex regulatory scheme to achieve the same social ends but through a means that is compatible with insurance markets composed of many competing firms.[1]

One is justifiably skeptical of a proposal for heavy regulation coming from the industry that is to be regulated. According to the economic theory of regulation first developed by the Nobel economist George Stigler, "As a rule, regulation is acquired by the industry and is designed and operated primarily for its benefit," as opposed to the

---

1. For additional discussion of the history and motivation behind these reform proposals, see Mark A. Hall, "The Political Economics of Health Insurance Market Reform," *Health Affairs*, vol. 11, no. 2 (Summer 1992), pp. 108–24.

idealistic view that regulation is "instituted primarily for the protection and benefit of the public at large."[2] This Stiglerian view characterizes public lawmaking as a crass economic good that can be bought and sold in the political marketplace. It suggests a raw abuse of government authority that co-opts sovereign power for private ends. In the words of another theorist, "There is essentially a political auction in which the high bidder receives the right to tax the wealth of everyone else."[3] Thus, the insurance industry might be charged with promoting regulation for anticompetitive reasons, in order to suppress price discounting or product enhancement.

But this negative view is not always accurate. In theory at least, the industry's self interest can coincide with the larger public interest. Certainly, the industry may go too far by advocating a form of regulation that is more conducive to its private interests than to those of the public, but individual and collective interests might both benefit from a dampening of excessive competition in some fashion.

Judging from the rapid reception of insurance market reforms in both state and federal legislatures, this appears to be such a happy case. It is surprising that, with the rest of the health care reform debate fracturing into countless ideological and interest groups, the basic structure of the industry's reform proposal is receiving broad political support. The proposal is contained in virtually every piece of federal reform legislation except single-payer proposals, and some elements have been enacted in all but eight states. Almost half the states have adopted the full slate of reforms. It is therefore imperative to understand precisely what these market reform proposals will and will not accomplish.

The Content of the Reform Proposals

The critical factor distinguishing this set of reforms from the broader reforms contained in pending federal proposals is that they function within a market for voluntary purchase. States encounter legal obstacles under the Employment Retirement Income Security Act (ERISA) in mandating employers' purchase of health insurance. Moreover, some conservatives oppose mandatory purchase requirements because of potentially negative economic consequences (increased unemployment if employers are required to purchase; increased taxes if

---

2. George Stigler, "The Theory of Economic Regulation," *Bell Journal of Economics and Management Science*, vol. 2 (Spring 1971), pp. 3–21.

3. Sam Peltzman, "Toward a More General Theory of Regulation," *Journal of Law and Economics*, vol. 19 (1976), p. 211–40.

they must subsidize individual purchase). At both ends of the political spectrum, however, some version of these proposals is regarded as necessary in any reform package—whether comprehensive or incremental, mandatory or voluntary—that relies on the private market.

The Scope of the Reforms. State legislative activity has focused on shoring up the small-group health insurance market. Some states have gone further, however, to extend these reforms to the individual market or to craft additional components not proposed by the insurance industry. The industry defines the small-group market as employers with three to twenty-five full-time workers.[4] Others go as high as fifty or a hundred. Setting an upper limit on the size of groups covered is intended to prevent the regulatory burden created by these reforms from further increasing the incentive of larger groups to self-insure. Cutting off the size at three is intended to demarcate the regulation of individual policies from group policies. If the individual market were opened to the favorable rating provisions in these reforms, a much larger group of bad risks might be pooled with the small group market, making reform of that market even more difficult. Under this view, the individual market should be addressed separately with high-risk pools and purchasing subsidies.

Although small-group market reforms vary considerably in their details, they share four essential components: (1) open enrollment and continuity of coverage; (2) rating bands and community rating; (3) private reinsurance; and (4) purchasing cooperatives. The NAIC's legislative model will serve as the basis for most of the following description.

Open Enrollment and Continuity of Coverage. The starting point of reform is to make sure that any willing purchaser has access to insurance and can retain that insurance through subsequent renewal

---

4. One dilemma to be resolved is how to treat associations of individuals or employers under this law. Excluding trade associations and MEWAs would create an opportunity for circumvention by allowing low-risk subscribers to purchase insurance for less than the rating bands described below. Including associations formed for the purpose of offering insurance, however, would allow adverse selection by individual subscribers against the small-group pool. California initially excluded associations, but it now includes very large trade associations (those with more than 1,000 members) along with small employers. Connecticut initially declared "fictitious groupings" of employers to be invalid, but it more recently amended its law to recognize the validity of small employers grouping together.

periods. Open enrollment, otherwise known as guaranteed availability or guaranteed issue, requires all insurers who participate in the small group market to accept any applicant. Guaranteed issue, which would require all insurers to offer open enrollment, differs slightly from guaranteed availability, which would require only the largest insurers in each state to do so but would encourage others to elect this role. Although coverage would always be available under the latter, not every insurer would have to issue it. New insurance companies could therefore enter the market more gradually.

Another variation, not yet adopted, is an allocation system like that used in many states for auto insurance. Allocation would allow any insurer to refuse an applicant but would then distribute all declined applicants evenly to insurance companies in proportion to their market shares. This approach has proved so unpopular for auto insurance that there is little support for its application to health insurance.

Under open enrollment, no group may be denied a minimum benefits health plan, regardless of its health status. Minimum benefits would be pared down by eliminating or overriding state-mandated benefit laws. Most proposals also call for a standard benefits plan, one that is more generous. Open enrollment is coupled with a whole-group concept, which requires all individuals within a group to purchase insurance if the group is to qualify for protection. This requirement prevents employers from angling for lower cost policies by excluding unhealthy employees and minimizes the selection problems that result if healthier workers drop out of the risk pool and purchase individual insurance.

Continuity of coverage is provided in three ways. First, insurers would be prohibited from refusing to renew insurance except for fraud, nonpayment, or similar malfeasance. Insurance theory tells us that, once good and bad risks are pooled randomly and a fair premium is set, insurers need not drop the bad risks when claims begin to accrue. The natural progression of losses does not destabilize the market. Just the opposite is true. The attraction of insurance is lost if it is sold only to those who make no claims and is revoked for those who use it after having paid premiums for years. If insurance does not remain available when the need arises, it is attractive neither to the sick nor to the healthy.

The second aspect of continuity is to regulate the use of preexisting condition exclusion clauses. Insurers would be prohibited from excluding any specific health conditions altogether (such as diabetes or cancer). They would be allowed only to place an initial twelve-month preexisting exclusion on all conditions manifested within six

35

months before the date of coverage or, under some proposals, only a six-month exclusion for conditions that existed during the prior three months. Some form of preexisting exclusion is necessary in a voluntary purchase market in order to counteract the tendency of subscribers to delay purchase until they are sick. A twelve- or six-month exclusion period is deemed sufficient rather than the periods of two years or longer that had come into use.

Third, these reforms address the problem of job lock, which arises when employees are afraid of undergoing an additional exclusion period if they change jobs. The reforms promote insurance portability by providing that subscribers, once enrolled, can transfer coverage to a new insurer, either by changing jobs or by changing insurers within the same workplace, without undergoing a new exclusion period, so long as the gap in coverage does not exceed one to three months.

Again, the logic is that of adverse selection. If insurance is being acquired in a setting that is demonstrably not driven by selection concerns—such as a change of job—risks should distribute themselves evenly and predictably. Therefore no special protection against adverse selection is necessary. Insurers can cover their risks simply by setting the initial premium appropriately. Some academic researchers have suggested that subscribers who switch insurance are higher risks than average (that is, they switch to increase their benefits when they are most in need).[5] According to the insurance industry's proposal, however, the differentiation between switchers and stayers, if any, is not severe enough to penalize switching. Easing the ability to switch is obviously critical to allowing insurers to compete on the basis of price and service quality.

Rating Bands. Open enrollment and continuity of coverage eliminate the worst effects of medical underwriting—refusal of coverage (blacklisting and redlining), job lock, and churning—but, standing alone, they would aggravate price variations and fluctuations by forcing insurers to take on the most extreme risks and allowing them to price their policies accordingly. The second component of the reforms is therefore to construct a variety of rating bands that compress the degree of price variation for small groups. These rating bands would

---

5. See Michael J. Goodman, Douglas W. Roblin, Mark C. Hornbrook, and John P. Mullooly, "Persistence of Health Care Expense in an Insured Working Population," in Mark C. Hornbrook, ed., *Advances in Health Economics and Health Services Research: Risk-Based Contributions to Private Health Insurance*, vol. 12 (Greenwich, Conn.: JAI Press 1991), pp. 149–76.

(1) restrict the amount insurers could increase the price for a single group over a span of time and (2) compress the range of prices across the market as a whole at a point in time.

The NAIC proposal limits year-to-year premium increases for any given group to 15 percent above the insurer's trend. Some proposals go even further by disallowing any annual increases beyond the market trend. This allows marketwide cost increases that are driven by technology advances, inflation in the medical sector, and the like (the trend) but limits increases that reflect group-specific health risk. (The market trend is measured by each insurer's increase in its least expensive new business. This measure, which allows some variation among insurers to reflect the effects of competition in holding down costs, is based on the theory that new business is the most competitive and therefore reflects market conditions more truly than does old business.)

The second component of the rating reforms would prevent any insurer from varying its prices among different small groups at any point more than 25 percent above or below its midpoint for groups with similar benefits and case characteristics.[6] This limit is imposed at the low end as well as the high end to lessen an insurer's incentive to engage in cherry picking or cream skimming by offering deep discounts to highly favorable groups.

The critical aspect of rate compression is not only the allowable width of each rating band (which ranges in different proposals from zero to plus or minus 35 percent), but also the number of rating bands that are permitted and the degree of variation among their midpoints. Under the industry's proposals, separate rating bands may exist for any combination of the following factors: geographic, demographic (age, sex), scope of benefits, and employer industry. The only limit on pricing variation across bands is that industry factors cannot account for more than a 30 percent spread (plus or minus 15 percent).

Proposals that allow separate blocks of business add another layer of complexity. Traditionally, many private insurers have treated all small group business as a single block (or book or class) of business for purposes of rating, product design, and marketing. Some have maintained distinct blocks, however, when their products are sold through separate sales forces, when they are acquired from

---

6. Observe that, during the first year of implementation, this limit can create a conflict with the restriction on annual increases for those insurers with existing wide spreads who would be forced to raise the rates at the low end of their rating bands more than the 15 percent annual increase limit.

another carrier, or when they have a fundamentally different design, such as HMO versus indemnity products. Most proposals follow the NAIC model by applying the rating limits separately to a limited number of blocks defined in this manner. To prevent circumvention of the rating limits by block gerrymandering (for example, defining a block as all the older work forces), these proposals limit the pricing variation among block mid-points to a 20 to 40 percent spread. The NAIC model permits unconstrained demographic rating within each block. Thus, even though each block's midpoint must be within a limited range of other blocks' midpoints, each block is allowed to contain an unlimited number of rating bands arrayed according to the demographic factors mentioned earlier.

Because of the flexibility among (as opposed to within) these rating bands, these reforms could allow more than a tenfold difference in the rates charged two small groups at either end of the possible combinations of risk factors, although such distant outliers might be very rare. For instance, if the HIAA reforms were applied to an insurance policy with an average annual cost of $1,500 (single coverage) per enrollee, a group of three healthy twenty-eight-year-old male computer software engineers in Vermont might pay only $1,865 a year while a group of three sickly fifty-eight-year-old male physicians in Boston might pay $30,555.[7]

Insurers almost certainly will have to live with some greater degree of rate compression than is contained in the model legislation if they want to present a workable reform package. Possibilities include: (1) setting outer limits on the allowable variation; (2) limiting the degree of variation that can result from specified component factors, much as the NAIC model now limits industry factors to a 30 percent spread; and (3) setting the reinsurance price to limit a carrier's exposure for demographic outliers, which would remove the incentive to use widely varying rating factors.

Community Rating. What many insurers, even many Blue Cross plans, oppose most vehemently is the requirement of pure community rating contained in several proposals and recently implemented (or being phased in) by Maine, New York, New Jersey, and Washing-

---

7. See Mark A. Hall, "Reforming the Health Insurance Market for Small Businesses," *New England Journal of Medicine*, vol. 326 (1992), pp. 565–70. See also American Academy of Actuaries, "Health Risk Assessment and Health Risk Adjustment: Crucial Elements in Health Care Reform," May 1993, p. 34 (NAIC rating bands allow an almost twelvefold variation at the outermost possible extremes).

ton.[8] New York's community rating law, for instance, requires that insurers offer the same rate to all subscribers for individual, small group (up to fifty), and Medicare supplemental insurance, allowing rates to vary only according to these three categories, to family status, and to covered benefits in each of nine regions in the state. No premium variation is allowed for health status, age, or industry group.

Advocates of community rating see the universe of potential purchasers falling into two camps: those who do not purchase because they are too poor or sick and therefore need a subsidy, and those who can afford insurance and therefore will continue to purchase as long as the rates are reasonable. The goal of community rating is to create an implicit subsidy for high-risk subscribers sufficient to enable the nonpoor to purchase, while maintaining enough low-risk subscribers to keep the average rates reasonable.

In a market of voluntary purchase, however, community rating has severe feasibility problems because it encourages younger, healthier groups and individuals to avoid purchasing insurance or to self-insure. Refusing to allow insurers to price these better risks accurately drives them from the risk pool, leaving only higher-than-average risks to support the pool. Then, when the pool's average community rate increases even further, still more members drop out, setting up a classic adverse selection spiral that could destroy the market entirely.[9]

As a result, states that have adopted pure community rating have experienced trouble with some commercial insurers withdrawing from the market or failing to offer affordable products to the market, particularly when community rating is applied to the market for individual insurance. In New York, for instance, commercial insurers offer no reasonably priced standard-coverage policies in the individual market, and in many locations the only real choice for individual subscribers is among HMOs.[10] In New Jersey, Blue Cross is the

---

8. Other states approach strict community rating by allowing only modest variation from a flat community rate but still less variation than would exist if insurers were allowed to rate according to age. These states include Louisiana, Florida, Maryland, Massachusetts, Oregon, and Vermont.

9. Other objections to community rating, from both an ethical and a feasibility perspective, are discussed in chapter 4. Included in that discussion is the important objection that community rating will be unfair among competing insurers, which is perhaps the strongest motivation for insurers' opposition.

10. Greg Steinmetz, "Eight Insurers End Individual Policies in New York State," *Wall Street Journal*, February 5, 1993. The individual policies offered

only insurer offering a range of reasonably priced options to the community-rated individual market.[11] Both states, however, have an ample supply of companies competing for the small-group market, as does Vermont, which also employs community rating.

Skeptics of adverse selection sometimes object that there is no hard or even anecdotal evidence that adverse selection would be a serious problem for health insurance, at least to the extent of destroying the market.[12] They reason that health insurance, unlike life or disability income insurance, which are discretionary, is too vital to be subject to intensive selection bias.

Experience shows, however, that adverse selection problems created by community rating are real. Adverse selection forced Blue Cross to abandon community rating in favor of experience rating for groups, and it is now destroying the market for individual and small-group insurance as subscribers select against the Blue Cross community-rated pools. Adverse selection has impeded the development of a significant market in private long-term health care insurance, since younger people with little need decline to purchase, and older subscribers cannot afford the high premiums.[13]

The pronounced effect of adverse selection on ordinary health insurance is borne out by the experience under the federal law (the Consolidated Omnibus Budget Reconciliation Act of 1985, known as COBRA) that allows employees to pay for continued group coverage for eighteen months after leaving a job. Employers and insurers report that COBRA continuation coverage produces claims that range from one-third to twice as high as for other group enrollees.[14] This is consistent with reports by insurers in the individual and small group market that premiums for medically underwritten coverage, which

---

by the only two commercial insurers participating either are extremely expensive (50–100 percent more than other plans) or have very high deductibles ($2,500–$5,000). Blue Cross offers reasonably priced fee-for-service options to individuals in some but not all parts of the state.

11. *BNA Health Care Daily*, August 5, 1993.

12. See, for example, Walton Francis, "A Health Care Program Run by the Federal Government that Works," *The American Enterprise*, vol. 4, no. 4 (July/ August 1993), p. 59; W. Allen and H. Ostrer, "Anticipating Unfair Uses of Genetic Information," *American Journal of Human Genetics*, vol. 53, no. 1 (July 1993), pp. 16–21.

13. Mark Pauly, "The Rational Nonpurchase of Long-Term-Care Insurance," *Journal of Political Economy*, vol. 98 (February 1990), pp. 153–68.

14. Gail A. Jensen, "Regulating the Content of Health Plans," in Robert B. Helms, ed., *American Health Policy: Critical Issues for Reform* (Washington, D.C.: AEI Press, 1993), pp. 181, 188.

screens for adverse selection, are 40–50 percent less than for nonmedically underwritten guaranteed issue plans.[15]

Adverse selection has also been a significant problem within larger groups that offer a choice among health plans, each of which carries the same group-community price. Because sick patients place more value on their established physician relationships and on their freedom to select their own specialists, they are more inclined than healthier and younger patients to select traditional, indemnity fee-for-service plans than HMOs. Sick patients also tend to select more generous benefits, and those with dental or mental health problems select insurance that covers those conditions.

These selection biases have been a continuing problem within the Federal Employees Health Benefits program, which covers most federal workers. Adverse selection resulted in the high-option (low-deductible) fee-for-service plan in one area attracting risks that were 50 percent higher than the plan's actuarial value based on standard risks, while the low-option (high-deductible) version of the same plan attracted risks that were about 40 percent lower than the plan's value based on standard risks.[16] According to another study, an insurer that offered two plans with the same actuarial value attracted subscribers with 79 percent higher claims to one than to the other.[17] As a consequence of these adverse selection problems, several fee-for-service plans and dozens of HMOs withdrew from FEHB during the late 1980s. Similar problems have plagued the California Public Employees Retirement System[18] as well as large private employers offering multiple options. In one study, a high-option plan attracted

---

15. Testimony presented to the NAIC Health Care Insurance Access Working Group, September 16, 1991, in Pittsburgh, Pa.; U.S. General Accounting Office, *Access to Health Insurance: State Efforts to Assist Small Businesses* (Washington, D.C.: Government Printing Office, May 1992), p. 24.

16. Although the risk-neutral value of the high-option plan was only 42 percent greater than the low-option plan, the actual costs (measured by experience-based premiums charged) for subscribers in the high-option plan were 264 percent higher. Marilyn J. Field and Harold T. Shapiro, eds., *Employment and Health Benefits: A Connection at Risk* (Washington, D.C.: Institute of Medicine, National Academy Press, 1993), p. 176.

17. Ibid. See also, M. Susan Marquis, "Adverse Selection with a Multiple Choice among Health Insurance Plans: A Simulation Analysis," *Journal of Health Economics*, vol. 11 (1992), pp. 129–51.

18. Harold Luft et al., "Adverse Selection in a Large Multiple-Option Health Benefits Program," in Richard Scheffler and Louis Rossiter, eds., *Advances in Health Economics and Health Services Research*, vol. 6 (Greenwich, Conn.: JAI Press, 1985), pp. 197–229.

enrollees that were as much as four times as expensive as those who chose the low-option plan from the same employer.[19]

The most successful attempt at community rating in a voluntary market is the one in Rochester, New York, where community rating prevails for about 85 percent of subscribers.[20] The Rochester market has several unique aspects, however. First, Blue Cross dominates the market, with 70 percent of the business, and it offers insurance only on a community-rated basis. The Blue Cross plan there has an unusual history, having been started by the business community, which itself is dominated by Eastman Kodak and a few other large employers. This market configuration allows a much higher level of community cooperation and voluntary health planning than in most other locations.[21] Blue Cross has negotiated aggressively for provider discounts that keep smaller insurance competitors from offering more favorable experience-based rates. Even then, erosion of community rating is setting in as some employers are beginning to self-insure or to demand experience-rated premiums.

As revealing as these examples are, they still illustrate selection against community-rated plans only when another form of insurance is available. There are no examples of adverse selection in a market that is entirely community-rated, which would require those opting out to go without insurance. Nevertheless, we know from experience in markets that are experience or risk rated that many average-to-good risk individuals and employers opt out because of the price of insurance. This tendency can only be aggravated by community rating, which will produce dramatic price increases for the youngest (and therefore lowest paid) groups and individuals.

In New York state, for instance, community rating was partially responsible for a 170 percent price increase by one large insurer for thirty-year-old males and a 30 percent increase for forty-five-year-old

---

19. R. P. Ellis, "The Effect of Prior-Year Health Expenditures on Health Coverage Plan Choice," in Scheffler and Rossiter, *Advances in Health Economics and Health Services Research*.

20. U.S. General Accounting Office, "Rochester's Community Approach Yields Better Access, Lower Costs" (Washington, D.C.: Government Printing Office, January 1993); William J. Hall and Paul F. Griner, "Cost-Effective Health Care: The Rochester Experience," *Health Affairs*, vol. 12, no. 1 (Spring 1993), pp. 58–69.

21. Compare the experience described by Larry Brown and Catherine McLaughlin in "Constraining Costs at the Community Level: A Critique," *Health Affairs* (Winter 1990), pp. 5–28.

males.[22] For group insurance, projections by Blue Cross, Aetna, and the American Academy of Actuaries based on existing business indicate that community rating would cause about 10 percent of small groups (fewer than twenty-five) to experience price increases of 40 percent or more and about 20 percent of groups would have increases of 20 percent or more.[23] These lower-risk subscribers would tend to drop out, while higher-risk subscribers would be drawn into the market, thereby increasing the community rate from its initial position, and so drive away even more low-to-average risks. The result, according to projections made by the Council for Affordable Health Insurance, is that pure community rating for individuals and small employers would cause a 25 percent increase in the average market premium and a 22 percent reduction in the total number of people insured.[24]

Much of this effect can be mitigated by allowing community rating by age, which produces increases of more than 20 and 40 percent respectively for only 4 percent and 2 percent of the existing individual and small group market.[25] To allow community rating by age differs little from allowing rating bands centered on age groups—the very industry-based proposals discussed above. This fallback position therefore concedes the argument that some variation in rates according to individual risk is desirable in a market of voluntary purchase. Whether risk is measured by age or by some

22. Henry Gilgoff, "Dialing in Desperation: Coming Change in Insurance Law Sparks Panic," *Newsday*, March 12, 1993. These increases also reflect underlying increases in the cost of care.

23. American Academy of Actuaries, "An Analysis of Mandated Community Rating," Washington, D.C., March 1993; William R. Jones, Charles T. Doe, and Jonathan M. Topodas, "Pure Community Rating: A Quick Fix to Avoid," *Journal of American Health Policy*, January/February 1993, pp. 29–33 (representing Aetna). See also Kenneth E. Thorpe, "Expanding Employment-based Health Insurance: Is Small-Group Reform the Answer?" *Inquiry*, vol. 29 (Summer 1992), pp. 128–36 (with move to community rating, 35 percent of groups would have price increases of 30 percent or more).

24. Victoria C. Craig, Mark Litow, and Greg Scandlen, "Mandatory Community Rating: The Most Dangerous Cure for Health Care Woes" (Alexandria, Va.: Council for Affordable Health Insurance, July 1993). Although this source, which represents small insurers, has a clear financial stake against community rating, its projections appear to be based on reasonable and documented assumptions about price increases and price sensitivity. The study is not explicit, however, about its price elasticity assumptions, and it does not elaborate on how sensitive the findings are to these assumptions.

25. American Academy of Actuaries, note 23.

degree of health status is largely a matter of detail.

Reinsurance. The third major component of the small-group market reforms is an industry-funded reinsurance pool for subscribers that are expected to generate costs exceeding the allowable premiums. Reinsurance encourages insurers to accept all applicants by allowing them to pass their worst risks to the reinsurance pool. This outlet suppresses the incentive to engage in risk selection in indirect and surreptitious ways, such as targeted marketing, gerrymandered benefit packages, selective poor service, or "losing" applications.

The principal funding for the reinsurance entity comes from the reinsurance premium paid by the ceding carrier. Carriers may prospectively reinsure either whole groups or high-risk individuals within groups. To reinsure high-risk groups, the NAIC calls for a premium of 150 percent of the marketwide average for a standard policy; to reinsure high-risk individuals, the price is 500 percent of the average market value for individuals within groups. These market averages would be determined by a reinsurance board and would be adjusted for the same coverage and demographic characteristics that determine rating bands.

Since insurers will reinsure only groups and individuals expected to have higher expenses than the allowable premiums, the reinsurance entity will suffer losses, which will be spread back to the insurance market through a premium tax on small-group business. The NAIC proposal calls for a limit of 5 percent; thereafter, other funding sources would be sought, such as large-group business, including self-insured employers, or possibly general revenues. These additional sources of funding would raise political and public policy concerns if insurers used the reinsurance option too aggressively. The experience is encouraging, however, in Connecticut, the first state to enact reinsurance. There, claims have not greatly exceeded premiums, so insurer assessments have been less than 2 percent of premiums.

A reinsurance mechanism for the small-group market differs in two ways from state high-risk pools that cover individual uninsurable persons. First, small-group reinsurance is invisible to the public. The decision to reinsure is made solely by the insurer when the policy is issued. The ceding company remains responsible for plan administration; the reinsurer merely indemnifies the issuing carrier for its claims expenses. Second, small-group reinsurance is a private mechanism, established as a nonprofit entity and funded primarily by the industry. (It is governed, however, by a quasi-governmental board.) This reinsurance mechanism also differs from conventional private reinsurance because it is used selectively for groups that are expected to be higher risks than the allowable premium reflects. In contrast, conventional reinsurance covers all of an insurer's risk pool for the unpredictable chance that an actuarially accurate premium will not be sufficient. Commercial reinsurance also does not have a redistributive funding mechanism.[26]

Reinsurance allows insurers to decide individually whether to keep the premium and assume the risk of a particular subscriber or forgo the premium and pass along the risk to the entire market. Without reinsurance, some companies would suffer the full brunt of bad risks above the rating bands, with no avenue for relief. Reinsurance also eliminates the need for intensive policing of tactics for gaming or circumventing the open enrollment and rate compression requirements. In essence, it creates an incentive-based system for controlling the worst effects of medical underwriting, thereby lessening the need to monitor the way the industry conducts its business. Indeed, even the rating limitations may be superfluous since, in a competitive market, the reinsurance price will tend to set a ceiling on the market price. Any insurer that charged substantially more than the reinsurance premium would lose business to competing insurers since they could charge slightly more than the reinsurance premium and still make a profit by ceding higher risks to the pool.

Reinsurance is subject to criticism, however, for minimizing the ceding carrier's incentive to control costs. HIAA calls for a transfer of the entire risk (less a $5,000 deductible for individuals), in order to encourage insurers to accept the highest-risk cases, but this transfer removes any incentive to manage care for the most expensive cases. Most states that have enacted reinsurance therefore include a substantial cost-sharing requirement or a much higher stop-loss threshold. The NAIC model, for instance, requires the ceding carrier to bear a $5,000 deductible in all reinsured cases plus 10 percent cost sharing for the next $50,000 of annual claims. Still, 10 percent may not be enough to encourage aggressive high-cost case management. The dilemma is that, if this cost-sharing percentage is raised further, it undermines the purpose of reinsurance, which is to relieve the insurer from bearing the costs of predictably higher-risk cases. The two goals of cost protection and cost sharing are difficult to reconcile because they are so fundamentally at odds.

Another difficulty arises from the disagreement among sectors

---

26. For an insightful discussion that makes many of these same points, see Randall R. Bovbjerg, "Reform of Financing for Health Coverage: What Can Reinsurance Accomplish?" *Inquiry*, vol. 29 (Summer 1992), pp. 158–75.

of the insurance industry over the structure of the reinsurance mechanism. For commercial insurers, reinsurance is the most critical component of reform, since it provides a private market mechanism for the equitable distribution of high-risk cases among many competing carriers. Thus, commercial insurers insist that reinsurance is essential to open enrollment and to their acceptance of pricing limitations that threaten the ability to engage in risk rating.[27]

HMOs hold a sharply contrasting view. A reinsurance mechanism does not fit well with the fully integrated HMO model epitomized by Kaiser-Permanente because it assumes a claims-based indemnity model of insurance in which the ceding carrier seeks reimbursement for particular claims from the reinsurance pool. Because many HMOs have no need to maintain fee-for-service pricing or cost-accounting structures, it is unclear how they are to submit claims. Moreover, HMOs view as unfair a proportional tax for the excess costs of reinsured claims when their managed-care techniques contribute lower-than-average costs to the pool. Other insurers assert that they too employ cost-minimizing managed-care techniques, that HMOs have lower costs because they attract healthier subscribers, and that HMOs cost more in any event because of their generous benefit packages.

Blue Cross takes an intermediate position on reinsurance. Some members favor reinsurance, but others who still offer open-enrollment and community-rated plans are accustomed to bearing high-risk cases internally and are less sophisticated at the underwriting analysis necessary to determine prospectively which customers to reinsure. An irony of reinsurance is that, while other reforms are designed to minimize medical underwriting, the reinsurance mechanism *rewards* insurers for their risk assessment talents. An insurer can beat its competition by better guessing which groups and individuals will incur costs greater than the reinsurance premium. Excessive reinsurance (passing off good risks) fritters away profits, while keeping too many risks will cause losses. The concern, then, is that commercial insurers with their powerful underwriting tools will gain an unfair competitive advantage from reinsurance. After Connecticut's adoption of an HIAA reform package, Blue Cross and Blue Shield of Connecticut, which traditionally did little medical

---

27. It is noteworthy, though, that in Vermont, where reinsurance was enacted after considerable argument, the commercial insurers have not yet pressured the Insurance Department to implement the pool. Vermont is a unique market, however, because it is dominated by Blue Cross and has a small area and population size.

underwriting, was reported to have invested $5 million in gearing up for reinsurance underwriting.

Blue Cross argues for several reinsurance alternatives. One is for reinsurance to be voluntary, that is, for each company to decide whether to go it alone, neither ceding any high risks nor contributing to the marketwide assessment. Blue Cross also advocates the option of "retrospective reinsurance." This is stop-loss coverage for groups or individuals that actually incur very large expenses, in contrast with first-dollar coverage for cases that insurers expect to be high cost.

Most proposals recognize these competing concerns of HMOs and Blue Cross by allowing a variety of reinsurance mechanisms and by permitting carriers that engage in community rating with open enrollment to opt out. Only six of the twenty-two states that have enacted reinsurance so far have made participation mandatory for all carriers. Making the reinsurance pool optional creates the complication, however, of needing to guard against insurers opting in only when their risk pools are higher than average. To deter gaming the reinsurance option, the NAIC model allows insurers to switch in or out of reinsurance only every five years.

Purchasing Cooperatives. In the insurance industry's words, the small-group market reforms discussed so far are aimed only at "availability, not affordability," meaning they are designed to offer insurance to any purchaser at prices not far above the market average; they are not intended to impose rate regulation or to reduce prices across the market. Insurers hope that focusing competitive pressures on the efficiency of medical care delivery will eventually lower prices, but in the short term the reforms will have just the opposite effect. These reforms will raise prices because they make insurance most attractive to the highest risk groups by holding prices to less than the policy's actuarial value. The excess is assessed against the premiums paid by all small-group purchasers, which will inevitably drive a number of low-risk purchasers out of the market, thus raising the market average even more.

The prospect that average prices will increase even more is of particular concern in a market of voluntary purchase. As mentioned above, one reason insurance is less prevalent among small groups than large ones is the much higher overhead cost that small-group purchasers face. Overhead costs are the portion of the premium that is not paid out in direct claims. There are three reasons why this portion is several times as high for smaller groups. First, the per enrollee cost of marketing a policy to smaller groups is much higher because it is spread over fewer people. These costs are compounded by the administrative expenses of medically underwriting small groups in order to counteract adverse selection. Second, smaller groups have less bargaining clout than large groups, so insurers can exact higher profits (although profit margins for all components of health insurance are quite low). Third, the risk premium for small groups is higher simply because the smaller risk pool minimizes the risk reduction created by the law of large numbers.

As a partial solution to these diseconomies of scale, several states and a number of academics have proposed creating purchasing cooperatives for the small group and individual markets. California, Florida, Iowa, Minnesota, North Carolina, Ohio, Texas, and Washington have already taken this step. These purchasing cooperatives go under several names, but health alliances or health insurance purchasing cooperatives (HIPCs) are the most common. Purchasing cooperatives were a cornerstone of the health care reform plan unveiled by President Bush during the 1992 campaign (under the name health insurance networks), and they are a centerpiece of President Clinton's health care reform plan, as well as of competing proposals from conservative Democrats and from Republican groups. The archetypal purchasing cooperative proposal was constructed by the Jackson Hole group, led by Alain Enthoven, Paul Ellwood, and Lynn Etheredge, and purchasing cooperatives served as the framework for California Insurance Commissioner John Garamendi's proposal for statewide universal coverage.[28]

Voluntary purchasing cooperatives have existed for years as multiple employer welfare arrangements (MEWAs). These MEWAs have garnered a tarnished reputation because of the mismanagement, bankruptcy, and outright fraud that occurred in a number of them. The current proposals for small group purchasing cooperatives differ, however, in several crucial respects. MEWAs are usually themselves insurers, not merely marketing services for other insurers. Their mismanagement occurred because many escaped regulation in the confusion over ERISA's preemption of state regulation of self-insurance.[29] More successful examples of purchasing cooperatives, sponsored by the Robert Wood Johnson Foundation, have operated in several demonstration sites.

The core idea of purchasing cooperatives for small groups and individuals is to give small employers more bargaining clout and to

---

28. See generally, *Health Affairs*, vol. 12, supp. (1993).

29. U.S. General Accounting Office, *States Need More Department of Labor Help to Regulate Multiple Employer Welfare Arrangements* (Washington, D.C.: Government Printing Office, GAO/HRD 92-40, March 1992).

streamline the marketing function by creating a larger risk pool. A purchasing cooperative contracts with a number of insurers who agree to offer their policies to small employers on a community-rated basis. A new entity—private, governmental, or quasi-governmental—can be created to perform this task, or small groups and individuals can piggyback on the state employee system, which is an existing purchasing network of considerable size.

Purchasing cooperatives create several advantages for both small employers and insurers. First, they minimize the search costs for small employers and the marketing costs for insurers. Small employers cannot afford to hire benefits managers, and insurers have to exert much greater effort to attract the attention of small-firm managers, who are often too busy to attend to the complexities of health insurance. Purchasing cooperatives help give the small-group market the expertise and economies of scale available to larger employers.

Second, purchasing cooperatives offer individual employees within small groups a menu of choices equal to or better than that given to employees of large firms. Small employers that offer insurance usually select only a single option, usually one that is not a managed-care plan. Purchasing cooperatives provide small-group employees access to a full range of insurance options.

Third, a purchasing cooperative can wield considerable market clout on behalf of its members. And finally, depending on the rate mechanism a purchasing cooperative chooses, it can have the effect of creating a much larger risk pool, causing an even greater compression of rates than do the rating bands discussed above. Most purchasing cooperative proposals call for strict or age-adjusted community rating, while others allow the full breadth of rating bands proposed by the industry.

The working model of a purchasing cooperative that is most frequently cited is the Council of Smaller Employers (COSE, pronounced "cozy"), which has operated successfully in Cleveland for two decades under the sponsorship of a local business association. COSE, which covers almost 150,000 people, has limited premium increases over a five-year period to about one-third of the trend for other small business in the area, and its administrative expenses are less than 12 percent of premiums, compared with an average of 27 percent for the small group market. COSE offers twelve health plans, ten of which are provided by Blue Cross.[30] Reports have also been

---

30. U.S. General Accounting Office, *Access to Health Insurance*; National Health Policy Forum, "Multiple Employer Purchasing Groups (METs, MEWAs, HINs, HIPCs): The Challenge of Meshing ERISA Standards with Health Insurance Reform," Issue Brief No. 604 (Washington, D.C., 1992).

encouraging on California's state-sponsored purchasing cooperative for small employers, established in mid-1993. It has received a strong surge of applications, and it negotiated adjusted community rates 6–23 percent less than the highly competitive rates available from the California Public Employees Retirement System (CalPERS), despite the anticipation of some adverse selection.[31] Florida's new purchasing cooperatives received initial bids 10–40 percent less than the prevailing market.

Other examples of purchasing cooperatives with successful track records come from the public sector. The Federal Employees Health Benefits (FEHB) program had a ten-year average increase in costs per enrollee of 9 percent a year despite an aging work force,[32] a figure that compares favorably with the double-digit increases in the private sector over the same period. Even more promising, CalPERS held premium increases to 1.4 percent in 1993 and to 6.1 percent the year before, and in 1994 it achieved a 1.1 percent rate rollback.[33]

Purchasing cooperatives are not included in the insurance industry's reform proposals (although the industry is formulating a version of purchasing cooperative legislation that is more acceptable to it than are others). Some commercial insurers, particularly smaller ones, are concerned that cooperatives are likely to narrow the market for small groups by selecting only a limited number of plans for inclusion. Insurers are also concerned that, in being required to deal with employees on an individual rather than a group basis, they will suffer from the biased selection effects discussed in the next chapter.

Changing to a system that offers a range of insurers rather than a single plan will fundamentally change the dynamics and perhaps the makeup of the insurance industry in a manner that favors larger insurers. Employers with a single plan are more likely to select traditional indemnity, which is all that small insurers typically offer. Large insurers are better able to form the managed-care options that purchasing cooperatives seek to offer. The second fundamental

---

31. *BNA Health Law Reporter*, May 27, 1993, p. 684; *BNA Health Care Daily*, March 7, 1994.

32. Walton Francis, "A Health Care Program Run by the Federal Government that Works," *The American Enterprise*, vol. 4, no. 4 (July/August 1993), pp. 50–61.

33. *BNA Health Care Policy Report*, March 8, 1993, p. 21. See also Roger Feldman and Bryan Dowd, "The Effectiveness of Managed Competition in Reducing the Costs of Health Insurance," in Robert B. Helms, ed., *Health Policy Reform: Competition and Controls* (Washington, D.C.: AEI Press, 1993), pp. 176–217 (reporting results from the program for Minnesota state employees).

change in market dynamics is the switch from wholesale to retail marketing. Purchasing cooperatives sometimes require insurers to market to individual employees rather than selling to employers in bulk. As a result of annual open enrollment, it will be much easier for employees to select new plans based on minor differences in costs or benefits, whereas before the entire group would have had to select new insurance. Some insurers see this much more fluid market as threatening their ability to compete.

These concerns over increased choice and the possibility of exclusion from the market are not fundamentally different, however, from the manner in which insurers now deal with very large employers. Small insurers have the greatest concerns because they have achieved a market niche by offering a single type of coverage to a limited segment of the market. For consumers, these changes represent an improvement in the market.

A greater problem is biased selection between the purchasing cooperative and the rest of the market (as distinct from biased selection among insurers within the cooperative, which can be controlled using the risk-adjustment techniques discussed in the next chapter). If purchasing cooperatives only offered a price advantage due to economies of scale, good and bad risk groups would have equal reasons to shop for insurance there. If cooperatives also adopt different rating rules from the rest of the market, however, they are certain to attract a disproportionate number of higher risk groups that will be favored by rate compression. Unless the purchasing cooperative's efficiencies are large enough to offset its increased risk profile, the resulting increase in rates will drive healthier groups back into the regular market. This will set off an adverse selection spiral unless the cooperative is allowed to screen out bad risks or to establish different risk pools with different prices.

COSE, for instance, was forced by the natural effects of adverse selection to create a separate pool for high-risk groups applying for membership and to turn down 20 percent of applicants. Thus, COSE has maintained its success in holding down costs partly by refusing high-risk groups. Kaiser, for instance, calculated that its COSE business was 5 percent less risky than its non-COSE small-group business.[34] State-sponsored cooperatives will not have this advantage.

The start-up of the California small group purchasing cooperative has been more successful because the rating method used inside the

---

34. U.S. General Accounting Office, *Access to Health Insurance*, p. 54; National Health Policy Forum, *Multiple Employer Purchasing Groups (METs, MEWAs, HINs, HIPCs)*.

cooperative pool allows for age-based risk adjustment, so it does not differ dramatically from the rating reforms applied to the rest of the market. Moreover, the California pool has negotiated very advantageous rates that remain attractive to healthy groups despite the somewhat greater compression in its rates.

Other states have tried to solve the selection problem by using the existing public employee insurance system as a small-group purchasing cooperative. Adding small groups to a large, stable pool of healthy government employees will help dampen the effects of adverse selection, as compared with a pool that consists of self-selected small groups. However, this may cause the community rate for the government employee pool to increase. As a consequence, state and local governments may have to raise additional public revenues or reduce benefits to government workers to pay for the implicit subsidy that this pool gives to private sector employees, neither of which is a happy solution. So far, however, state employee insurance pools that have allowed local governments to opt in have not had serious adverse selection problems.[35]

There are two remedies for market selection problems created by purchasing cooperatives. One is to apply the same rating reforms both inside and outside the cooperatives, placing cooperative insurers on more even footing with the rest of the market. Outside insurers are then forced to compete with the prices established within the cooperative, which extends the benefits of the cooperative's economies of scale. Voluntary cooperatives with uniform rating rules also allow the cooperative concept to prove itself by market performance rather than forcing the entire market into an untested new system.

A second method for reducing selection problems is to make small employers, if they wish to purchase insurance, do so through the cooperative. Naturally, exclusive cooperatives will escalate insurers' concerns over market exclusion. If purchasing cooperatives are not exclusive, however, insurers can continue the duplicative marketing efforts that contribute to the higher costs cooperatives are intended to eliminate. Furthermore, nonexclusive purchasing cooperatives already exist in about 150 cities in almost every state (in the form of MEWAs) by virtue of natural market forces and voluntary cooperation among employers.[36] If cooperatives are not made the exclusive source of insurance, it is not clear that authorizing legislation creates any innovation beyond what the market can produce

---

35. Richard Kronick, "Managed Competition—Why We Don't Have It and How We Can Get It," in Helms, *American Health Policy*, p. 58.

36. U.S. General Accounting Office, *Access to Health Insurance*, p. 52.

on its own operating under the guaranteed issue and rating rules discussed above.

Another way selection problems manifest themselves is at the borders of the regulated market. Restricting the cooperative to small groups creates border-policing problems similar to those described at the beginning of this chapter. Large employers with older or unhealthy work forces who are already purchasing insurance on their own will have an incentive to divide their work forces into artificially smaller groups so that the riskier workers can be sent to the community-rated pool. This gerrymandering of corporate subsidiaries obviously creates a selection problem and is unfair to the small-group pool since the healthy component of the larger employer market does not contribute to the pool. This strategy will therefore have to be monitored.

The Effects of Small-Group Market Reforms

The Good News. Small-group market reforms are designed to accomplish two efficiency objectives. First, they induce insurers to behave more consistently with the fundamental premises of group insurance by minimizing individual medical underwriting. Rather than imposing laborious regulatory oversight of discrete underwriting techniques such as blacklisting, cherry picking, and churning, the private reinsurance mechanism achieves this goal through an incentive-based system. The reinsurance mechanism encourages the industry to assume all risks while assessing it for the costs of higher risks passed on to the reinsurance pool. Second, these reforms help to reorient the industry from competition based on risk selection to competition based on risk management.

As discussed in chapter 2, insurers of conventional risks, such as life, fire, liability, and the like, compete primarily on the basis of risk selection, not risk management. Liability insurers do not attempt to design products for their manufacturing clients, and homeowner's insurers do not build houses. These decisions are made by subscribers, leaving to insurers only the task of measuring the risk effects of those decisions. More accurate risk pricing serves the social objective of imposing on subscribers the costs of their own risk-generating activities. This places the risk management incentive with the party in the best position to take protective measures. Thus, for traditional lines of insurance, underwriting serves to minimize social losses by inducing subscribers to optimize their risk reduction efforts. Risk assessment also enhances social welfare by counteracting adverse selection with refinements in risk segmentation. Finally, risk selection also counters moral hazard by preventing subscribers from imposing the costs of their risk-increasing behavior on others. In other words, conventional insurance works best the more nearly that insurance is accurately risk-rated.

Health insurance differs fundamentally because we are not willing to countenance widespread decisions not to purchase it. Risk selection in health insurance has counterproductive effects if it makes insurance unaffordable (albeit accurately priced) for some portion of the population. Health insurance has assumed the social function of a financing mechanism for predictable costs as well as a risk-pooling function for unexpected costs. The social goal is payment for care through the claims process rather than the signaling of costs to subscribers by premium variations. Therefore, the very activity that enhances social welfare for conventional insurance—more accurate screening of risks—tends to undermine the social function of health insurance by pricing it out of reach of a segment of the population.

Health insurers can contribute to social welfare, first, by insuring as broadly as possible, and, second, by actively managing the risks they insure. Management takes the form of policing the costs of care through provider controls imposed collectively on behalf of their subscribers. At the same time, some price variability is desirable since individual subscribers do control to some degree their health risks and attendant costs of treatment. Therefore, some risk rating facilitates competitive pressures to manage health care costs. Some risk segmentation may also be necessary for purely logistical reasons. The smooth functioning of a competitive market that gives consumers a range of choices among insurance options requires some adjustment for risk among insurers. Small-group market reforms attempt to balance these competing objectives by guaranteeing open enrollment and continuity of coverage but allowing limited price variation. The result is to minimize underwriting and risk selection in favor of competition based on efficiency in the delivery of medical care.

The Bad News. Despite these considerable benefits, small-group market reforms, as now structured, will not achieve the fundamental goals of health care reform to the extent the industry would hope. Insurance can be said to be accessible to high-risk groups only to the extent that its price does not vary dramatically from the average. The rating bands advocated by the industry, however, allow too much variability to make insurance affordable to small groups of older or unhealthy workers.

Rating restrictions can be made more severe, as several states have done and as some federal bills have proposed, by moving toward pure community rating. But community rating is difficult to administer in a voluntary market for the reasons discussed above.

Even if some workable compromise can be found for the rate compression problem, these reforms will not enhance access to the extent the industry would hope; indeed, as several observers have argued, they may decrease the prevalence of private insurance.[37] Some highly publicized cases of insurance denial for small employers may involve firms desperate to purchase at any reasonable price, but most of the working uninsured apparently do not fall into this category.

Several surveys have demonstrated that only a minority, and perhaps a very small minority, lack insurance because they have an uninsurable condition or can obtain only substandard coverage. The congressional Office of Technology Assessment questioned seventy-three commercial insurers in 1988 and found that about three-quarters of all individual and small-group applicants are offered coverage at standard rates. Of the remaining applicants, 15 to 20 percent are offered substandard coverage, which usually means a permanent exclusion of preexisting conditions but sometimes means standard coverage at rates 50 percent or more higher than the norm for a given age group. Commercial insurers deny only 8 percent of individual applicants.[38] Because applicants who are likely to be turned down usually apply to more than one company, these figures represent the maximum of uninsurable individuals. A lower estimate comes from the 1987 National Medical Expenditure Survey, which questioned individuals, not insurers. According to those data, only 2.5 percent of those without insurance have been denied standard coverage at standard rates.[39] This level of uninsurable applicants could easily be absorbed by existing high-risk pools in twenty-six states or by Blue Cross plans that maintain open enrollment and

37. T. A. Lyle, "The False Promise of Small-Group Reform," *Emphasis*, no. 1 (1991), pp. 2–4; U.S. Congress, House, Subcommittee on Health of the Committee on Ways and Means, *Hearings on Standards for Private Health Insurance*, 102d Cong., 1st sess., May 21, 1991, statement of Mark V. Nadel, of the Government Accounting Office; ibid., May 2, 1991, statement of Harry Sutton, of the American Academy of Actuaries.

38. U.S. Congress, Office of Technology Assessment, "Medical Testing and Health Insurance" (Washington, D.C.: Government Printing Office, August 1988).

39. Karen Beauregard, *Persons Denied Private Health Insurance Due to Poor Health*, Agency for Health Care Policy and Research publication no. 92-0016 (Rockville, Md.: December 1991).

community rating in fourteen other states.[40]

For the most part, workers lack insurance because it is too expensive for employers to offer, even at average rates. Some employers may be unwilling to purchase insurance even at prices far below market averages. In a nationally representative stratified sampling of more than 3,000 employers in 1990, HIAA found that labor market factors and underlying costs, not product availability, account for a large portion of firms not offering health insurance.[41] Only 30 percent of surveyed firms cited unavailability of an acceptable plan as a very important reason for not purchasing insurance, while three-quarters cited expense and over half cited low profits as very important. Firms without health insurance have nearly three times as many employees earning less than $10,000 as do firms with insurance (33 percent compared with 12 percent). Employers also tend not to offer insurance for jobs with high turnover. The turnover rate for uninsured firms is three times the rate for insured firms (39 percent versus 13 percent). Similar findings are reflected in surveys conducted by the federal government, the National Federation of Independent Business, Robert Wood Johnson Foundation grantees, and Catherine McLaughlin and her associates.[42]

Insurers respond to these financial barriers by offering to strip away enough benefits to make insurance affordable. Thirty-one states have enacted so-called bare-bones laws on the basis of research showing that state mandated-benefit laws add 10–20 percent to the

---

40. Randall R. Bovbjerg, "Comprehensive Health Insurance Pools after Fifteen Years: A Current Policy Perspective," report prepared for the Health Insurance Association of America (Washington, D.C.: November 1991); U.S. General Accounting Office, *Access to Health Insurance*, pp. 46–50.

41. C. Lippert, E. Wicks, *Critical Distinctions: How Firms That Offer Health Benefits Differ from Those That Do Not* (Washington, D.C.: Health Insurance Association of America, 1991, based on an HIAA 1990 employer survey).

42. Stephen H. Long and M. Susan Marquis, "Gaps in Employer Coverage: Lack of Supply or Lack of Demand?" *Health Affairs*, vol. 12 (1993 supplement), pp. 282–93; Charles P. Hall and John M. Kuder, *Small Business and Health Care—Results of a Survey* (Washington, D.C.: National Federation of Independent Business Foundation, 1990); Catherine G. McLaughlin and Wendy K. Zellers, "The Shortcomings of Voluntarism in the Small-Group Insurance Market," *Health Affairs*, vol. 11, no. 2 (Summer 1992), pp. 28–40; Catherine G. McLaughlin, "The Dilemma of Affordability—Health Insurance for Small Businesses," in Helms, *American Health Policy*, pp. 152–66; W. David Helms, Anne K. Gauthier, and Daniel M. Campion, "Mending the Flaws in the Small-Group Market," *Health Affairs*, vol. 11, no. 2 (Summer 1992), pp. 7–27.

cost of insurance.[43] These laws allow insurers to sell stripped down coverage to previously uninsured purchasers at greatly reduced prices. In most states, however, these efforts have been a dismal failure and have produced only a modest response in the best circumstances. The mandated benefits most subject to criticism—such as for acupuncture and chiropractic services—add little to the cost of insurance,[44] and the 10 percent savings produced by paring back most mandates[45] are not sufficient to attract many new subscribers. This range of savings is negated by only a single year of typical inflation. Insurers have therefore had to reduce prices by drastically limiting coverage through very high deductibles and copayments or very low payment limits. Some bare-bones policies cover only twenty days of hospitalization or cap benefits at $50,000 annually; others impose deductibles of $1,000 or more. This insurance package is so unattractive that few wish to purchase it despite its reasonable price. Most bare-bones states have sold no more than a few hundred policies, and some have sold only a few dozen or less. In some states that offer a standard package of benefits (Missouri, Oklahoma, Oregon, and Washington), the results have been more encouraging, although still modest, with policies covering several thousand subscribers.[46]

The second solution to the affordability problem is a subsidy that will encourage the purchase of adequate insurance coverage.[47] Other

---

43. Jensen, "Regulating the Content of Health Plans," pp. 167–93.

44. U.S. General Accounting Office, *Access to Health Insurance*, p. 32.

45. All mandates cannot be eliminated because those such as guaranteed renewability and continuity of coverage laws and laws requiring family policies to cover newborns despite their preexisting congenital defects are highly desirable and promote the goal of increased coverage.

46. See, generally, "No Sale: The Failure of Barebones Insurance" (Washington, D.C.: Families USA, July 1993); Susan Laudicina, *Impact of State Basic Benefit Laws on the Uninsured* (Washington, D.C.: Blue Cross and Blue Shield Association, December 1992); Patricia A. Butler, "Flesh or Bones? Early Experience of State Limited Benefit Health Insurance Laws" (Portland, Maine: National Academy for State Health Policy, August 1992).

47. For instance, the favored tax status of employer-provided health insurance premiums (namely, their exclusion from the employee's earned income) could be extended to purchasers of individual insurance. Voucher or tax-credit subsidies could also be given to firms with low-wage work forces. The difficulty in designing these subsidy mechanisms is to distinguish those who are able or willing to purchase without the subsidy from those who are not. A criterion that limits the subsidy to those who are not insured makes sense only in the short term and creates an incentive for those with insurance to drop coverage in order to qualify. Limiting the subsidy to low-income groups

real-world tests suggest, however, that price-lowering effects would have to be extraordinarily large to work well in a voluntary market. A series of demonstration projects sponsored by the Robert Wood Johnson Foundation over three years has shown that uninsured small employers have a frustrating degree of resistance to buying even highly subsidized health insurance. Despite aggressive marketing efforts and purchasing cooperatives in some of the sites, as well as subsidies of one-quarter to one-half of market value, most demonstration sites achieved far less than 10 percent penetration of their target markets of previously uninsured small groups.[48] One-third of surveyed employers without insurance in Denver and one-fourth in Alabama said they would not contribute any amount toward their employees' health insurance.[49] Two pilot projects in New York found that, "at most, the proportion of [small, previously uninsured] firms offering insurance increased 3.5 percentage points" despite a 50 percent subsidy. Moreover, the evaluators concluded, "Nearly 60 percent of small firm owners still would not purchase insurance even with a 75 percent price subsidy."[50]

The problems caused by the insensitivity of uninsured employers to reductions in price are compounded by the high sensitivity to price among those who are insured. Price sensitivity among insured small employers is a matter for considerable concern because small-group

---

or individuals ignores the fact that health insurance is becoming unaffordable or undesirable even at middle incomes.

48. W. Helms, Gauthier, and Campion, "Mending the Flaws in the Small-Group Market," pp. 7–27.

49. U.S. Congress, House, Subcommittee on Health of the Committee on Ways and Means, *Private Health Insurance: Options for Reform*, Committee Print 101-35. September 20, 1990 (remarks by Judith Glazner, of Colorado, and Hugh Davis, of Alabama, at a seminar, "Health Insurance for the Uninsured: Strategies and Policy Options for a Public/Private Partnership," Washington, D.C., May 31, 1990). Another opinion survey found, however, that a price reduction of 50 percent would induce half of small firms now without insurance to purchase. Jennifer N. Edwards, Robert J. Blendon, Robert Leitman, Ellen Morrison, Ian Morrison, and Humphrey Taylor, "Small Business and the National Health Care Reform Debate," *Health Affairs*, vol. 11, no. 1 (Spring 1992), pp. 164–73.

50. These findings were probably biased, however, by severe restrictions on eligibility for the program. The firm owners were not allowed to participate personally or to require employees to pay any portion of the premium. K. Thorpe, A. Hendricks, D. Garnick, K. Donelan, and J. Newhouse, "Reducing the Number of Uninsured by Subsidizing Employment-based Health Insurance," *Journal of the American Medical Association*, vol. 267 (1992), pp. 945–48.

reforms raise average prices by drawing higher risks into the market. Actuarial simulations of the effect of various rating bands, performed for HIAA and Blue Cross based on data from existing insured groups, estimate an average increase in per capita claims ranging from 5 percent to 25 percent in the first year of reform.[51] The Society of Actuaries projects that guaranteed issue will result in claims costs increasing from the base year by about 20 percent in the first year, 50 percent in the second year, 25 percent in the third year, and 13 percent in the fourth year.[52]

Rate restrictions, in addition to attracting higher risks, make insurance more expensive for the lowest risks by compressing the differential between existing low- and high-risk groups. Some previously insured employers can therefore be expected to drop coverage, raising market averages even more. Subscribers are not priced out of the market only at the high end of the price range. As Mark Pauly observes, the willingness to pay for insurance varies with one's expected loss. Therefore, marginal price effects can be felt across the full range of risk-rated prices.[53]

How many lower-risk subscribers will drop coverage because of price increases depends on the price sensitivity among insured employers. Attempts to measure price elasticity using dissimilar methodologies have produced widely varying results.[54] Most economists conclude, however, that employers are fairly to highly price sensitive.[55] Using a conservative elasticity estimate of -2, a 10 percent increase in the price of insurance is likely to result in 20 percent of insured employers dropping coverage.

---

51. P. Anthony Hammond, *H.R. 3626 and Its Effects on the Small-Employer Market* (Washington, D.C.: Health Insurance Association of America, June 1992).

52. Society of Actuaries, *Variation by Duration in Small-group Medical Insurance Claims* (New York: Society of Actuaries, September 5, 1991).

53. Mark Pauly, "Fairness and Feasibility in National Health Care Systems," *Health Economics*, vol. 1 (1992), pp. 93–103.

54. We know, for instance, that workers switch plans to avoid minor costs, reflecting a high level of price sensitivity. Deep discounts in the cost of insurance, however, do not induce many uninsured employers to add coverage. This difference, if it is real, may reflect one of the following: (1) workers are more price sensitive than employers; (2) insured work forces are more price sensitive than uninsured ones; (3) price sensitivity varies widely, and these two observations come from opposite ends of the spectrum.

55. See Michael A. Morrisey, *Price Sensitivity in Health Care: Implications for Health Care Policy* (Washington, D.C.: National Federation of Independent Business Foundation, 1992), pp. 37–53.

Disenrolling low-risk groups may, of course, be offset by an even greater number of newly enrolling high-risk groups, but this is unlikely. First, projections show that the number of losers under various rating bands will far outnumber the number of winners, since many average risks must suffer a modest increase in order to lower the price for a few very bad risks. Under the rating bands considered in several bills during the 102d Congress, for instance, various projections predicted that four times as many subscribers would suffer price increases as would receive price reductions.[56] Moreover, even if winners and losers were better balanced, the sensitivity to price may be markedly different for currently insured versus currently uninsured employers: the former may be more likely to drop coverage than the latter are to add it, for a given price differential. Therefore, the HIAA estimate that tighter rating bands may decrease insurance purchase by 2–5 percent is probably conservatively realistic.[57]

The most dire projections have not been borne out, however, in states that first implemented small-group reforms. No dramatic price increases are reported in Connecticut, North Carolina, or Vermont, nor has there been a huge outcry from insured small employers. An American Academy of Actuaries survey in early 1994 of insurers in eleven reform states found much less market disruption than anticipated. Although two-thirds of insurers reported price increases, most attributed this to underlying trends, not to the reforms. Data are insufficient to determine whether the proportion of the population insured has gone up or down, but a cursory assessment is promising. Half the respondents in the American Academy of Actuaries survey reported an increase in the number of insured small groups, but 29 percent reported a decrease; neither group agreed on whether market reforms were the reason for these changes. In Connecticut, more than 5,000 plans were sold to previously uninsured small employers during the first two years under market reform.[58] In North Carolina, another early state with a full set of reforms, 7,300 new plans were issued in the first year of market reform, with 60 percent going to previously uninsured groups.[59] And, in California, where small-

---

56. Hall, "The Political Economics of Health Insurance Market Reform," pp. 108–24.

57. Hammond, *H. R. 3626 and Its Effects on the Small-Employer Market.*

58. Connecticut Small Employer Health Reinsurance Pool, *Market Place Report* (Hartford, Conn., May 1993). The report gives no data about the number of employers dropping coverage, so the net effect on the level of coverage cannot yet be determined.

59. Personal communication with Allen Feezor, chief deputy commissioner of insurance. There is no information on the rate of disenrollment during the same period.

group reforms took effect in mid-1993, insurance regulators report a strong surge of applications for new coverage.[60]

In sum, the working uninsured are composed primarily of two groups: high risks who cannot afford insurance, and low risks who cannot afford insurance. Small-group reforms will help the former and hinder the latter. It is impossible to gauge how these counteracting effects will net out over time, but it is possible that some form of adverse selection spiral may result in significantly fewer employers voluntarily purchasing insurance, although those purchasing will be sicklier and thus more needy. With or without a price spiral, however, it is certain that prices will not drop sufficiently to induce most small employers to purchase voluntarily. Therefore, the only way to produce universal insurance is to mandate its purchase by all employers or individuals.

---

60. *BNA Health Care Daily*, July 7, 1993.

4

Insurance Market Reform under a System of Mandatory Purchase

To focus on the aspects of insurance market reform of most relevance under a system of mandatory purchase, this chapter assumes that a system of mandatory purchase is in place. This premise avoids several major issues. It assumes the desirability of private over government insurance, and it does not deal with the larger questions of whether the mandate should be on individuals or employers, whether global budgeting is compatible with managed competition, or how mandatory purchase would be phased in or how much government subsidy should be provided. Instead, this analysis focuses on how the subscriber choice and premium pricing mechanisms can be structured to maximize the social benefits of a market among competing private insurers. Principally, this raises two issues: whether community rating is desirable, and how purchasing cooperatives should be operated.

Community Rating

The core issue for insurance market reform under a system of mandatory purchase is how insurance policies are to be priced to employers or individual subscribers. Most commentators favor as strict a version of community rating as possible. President Clinton's proposal, for instance, calls for health plans to offer the same price to every subscriber within each health alliance for each type of coverage. The few states that have moved toward mandatory purchase have required phased-in rate compressions that will eventually approach or reach pure community rating. New York state instituted an immediate system of pure community rating for small groups and individuals as part of its voluntary system reforms, and several other states are phasing in pure or nearly pure forms of community rating as part of their voluntary systems. Even former president George Bush's reform plan, which was a voluntary system, appeared to contemplate an eventual move to community rating.

Community rating requires each insurer to charge a single rate to all of its customers for a given level of coverage. Each insurer's price will therefore reflect the average costs to its community of subscribers for each type of policy. There are two versions of community rating. Strict, flat, or pure community rating is as just described. It allows an insurer to vary its price only according to geographic location, the content of the insurance policy, and the size of the subscriber unit (individual, spouse, or family). The alternative, called community rating by class or age-adjusted community rating, allows insurers to charge different community rates for different age groups. Typically, an insurer will create separate classes according to five-year increments. Age-adjusted community rating prevailed in the small-group market before the market started to collapse, and exists today in most Blue Cross plans that still use any version of community rating. Pure community rating was virtually abandoned long ago, and even community rating by class is becoming extinct because of the severe selection effects in a market of voluntary insurance. The issue here is whether some form of community rating can be resurrected in a market where everyone is required to purchase and every insurer is required to sell according to the same rules. This inquiry has two dimensions: whether community rating is fair and whether it is technically feasible. The latter requires an examination of methods for risk adjustment.

Tax Equity Arguments. Is community rating the fairest way to set insurance premiums for those above a defined poverty level? Assuming that no method would be allowed to impose a greater financial burden on any social class than it could bear, the question becomes, How should premiums be distributed across age, income, and health status groups? The answer depends on one's criterion of fairness. If equal burden for equal coverage is the criterion, then community rating is the fairest method. If equal burden for equal risk is the criterion, community rating is perversely unfair. The very purpose of community rating is to require lower-risk groups to subsidize higher-risk groups in direct disproportion to their risk.

If the criterion of fairness is to pay according to one's financial ability measured by income or wealth, then the result is cloudier. On its surface, community rating is regressive since, like a poll tax, it charges the same regardless of various abilities to pay above a poverty threshold. This regressivity is tempered by the fact that subscribers pay only a portion of the premium, ranging from 50 percent to 20 percent or less in various proposals (and depending on which insurance plan the subscriber selects). The remainder of the premium is paid either by the employer or through a tax-supported government subsidy, the fairness of which is determined by the contribution formula or the method of taxation.

The Clinton proposal contains a mixture of graduated, proportional, and regressive funding mechanisms. At the first cut, the portions paid by both the employer and the subscriber are community rated, which, as discussed below, can be viewed as regressive. Employers' contributions are capped, however, at a percentage of payroll (initially on a sliding scale but phasing into a uniform 7.9 percent cap), with tax revenue sources making up the difference. Low-income subscribers would also receive a subsidy from general revenues to help them afford the average-cost plan in each area. These other revenue sources divert savings from Medicare and Medicaid, which have both proportional and progressive financing systems, and they rely on corporate taxes, which are mostly proportional, and on "sin" taxes, which are nominally flat but have regressive economic effects.

The fairness of community rating is radically altered if one looks below its surface (the same amount for each person) and considers the implicit subsidization of unhealthy subscribers by healthy ones. As an implicit form of taxation, this subsidy effect is perversely unfair because younger workers tend to earn far less than do older ones. Community rating can therefore be characterized as taxing low-income workers to support high-income workers.

Roger Feldman and Bryan Dowd have estimated that community rating would result in families headed by persons under twenty-five years old paying about twice their actuarial value, and families from fifty-five to sixty-four paying only three-quarters of their actuarial value. This subsidy of several thousand dollars per family would flow from a group that earns $22,477 per year to one earning $47,852 a year in 1991.[1] David Bradford and Derrick Max roughly estimate that the Clinton plan would result in those aged twenty-five to thirty-four paying $26 billion more and those aged fifty-five to sixty-four paying $33 billion less, as compared with an entirely age-adjusted rating

---

1. Roger Feldman and Bryan E. Dowd, "Biased Selection—Fairness and Efficiency in Health Insurance Markets," in Robert B. Helms, ed., *American Health Policy: Critical Issues for Reform* (Washington, D.C.: AEI Press, 1993), pp. 64–86. Another study estimated that 12–33 percent of the premium for subscribers with actuarial costs below the average community rate goes to subsidize subscribers with above-average risks. Roger L. Pupp, "Community Rating and Cross Subsidies in Health Insurance," *Journal of Risk and Insurance*, vol. 48 (December 1981), pp. 610–27.

system.[2] Henry Aaron and Barry Bosworth observe that adopting community rating will produce a greater redistribution than choosing whether government, business, or individuals will pay. Their rough calculations indicate that community rating will require employers in some industries to pay as much as $2,000 more and $4,000 less per employee than at present.[3]

The risk-based view of fairness is a plausible one that, naturally, is advanced by the insurance industry.[4] In one nationally placed advertisement, the commercial insurance industry labeled as "unfair to everyone" any form of rating that fails to treat equally policyholders with the same risk, observing that "if insurance companies didn't put people into risk groups, it would mean that low-risk people . . . would have to pay higher rates" for someone else's bad habits. This risk-based view of fairness is captured in state insurance laws that would, for instance, deem it illegal and "unfair discrimination" to charge identical life insurance premiums to a sixty-year-old and a twenty-year-old.[5]

Community rating proponents respond that this libertarian view "confuses actuarial fairness with moral fairness." The philosopher Norman Daniels observes that other theories of justice such as that in John Rawls's powerful argument require society to care for the victims of nature's misfortunes.[6] We are born with genetic defects, trapped in environmental influences we cannot change, and struck with random accidents and infectious illnesses. Communitarian ethics say that we should contribute equally toward sharing society's collective burdens.[7]

---

2. David F. Bradford and Derrick Max, "Community Rating in Clinton's Health Reform: Another Hit to the Young?" (American Enterprise Institute working paper, November 16, 1993, draft). These numbers attribute the entire premium to individuals rather than deducting the employer share, under the assumption that employer contributions lower take-home pay.

3. Henry J. Aaron and Barry Bosworth, "Economic Issues in Reform of Health Care Financing," Brookings Institution (1993). These estimates are corroborated by Lewin-ICF, *Business and Health*, January 1994, p. 12.

4. William R. Jones, Charles T. Doe, and Jonathan M. Topodas, "Pure Community Rating: A Quick Fix to Avoid," *Journal of American Health Policy*, January/February 1993, pp. 29–33.

5. Kenneth S. Abraham, "Efficiency and Fairness in Insurance Risk Classification," *Virginia Law Review*, vol. 71 (1985), pp. 403–51.

6. Norman Daniels, "Insurability and the HIV Epidemic: Ethical Issues in Underwriting," *Milbank Quarterly*, vol. 68, no. 4 (1990), pp. 497–525.

7. Mark A. Hall, "Community Rating or Experience Rating?" *The Responsive Community*, vol. 2, no. 4 (Fall 1992), pp. 79–82; Deborah Stone, "The

Nevertheless, the very concept of a single rate for each community acknowledges the validity of at least one rating category— location. The fortuity of where one lives can cause prices to vary 100 percent or more simply because of the widely different costs of care between states and between rural and urban locations. Additional variation arises from the age demographics in different locations.

One counterargument to the risk-based view of the regressive subsidy in community rating is to view health risk over the span of each worker's life rather than at a moment in time. Younger workers may not be carrying an unfair burden if they will receive the benefits of the subsidy themselves when they are older, just as those who contribute now to social security will be its recipients later.

This longitudinal view fails to rehabilitate community rating, however. If we were to allocate our lifetime medical expenses, we probably would not favor an even burden over the different portions of our productive careers; instead, we would want a lower burden during our low-wage years and a higher burden later. Wages for males[8] increase approximately twofold over a career, tending to increase rapidly at the outset and to peak at around ages forty-five to fifty,[9] while male health risk varies from threefold to fourfold between young and old workers and increases more rapidly in later years.[10] The parallels between average health risk and average asset accumulation are even stronger, since wealth (net worth) varies five- to tenfold on average across age groups and tends to increase rapidly during one's forties and fifties.[11] Therefore, the preferred distribution

---

Struggle for the Soul of Health Insurance," *Journal of Health Politics, Policy and Law,* vol. 18, no. 2 (Summer 1993), pp. 286–317.

8. Both wages and health risk are flatter for females. The focus is on males because they are more likely to have an uninterrupted career and because they are frequently the principal wage-earner whose employer provides dependent coverage.

9. Bruce E. Kaufman, *The Economics of Labor Markets,* 3d ed. (Fort Worth: Dryden Press, 1991), p. 335; Kevin M. Murphy and Finis Welch, "Empirical Age-Earnings Profiles," *Journal of Labor Economics,* vol. 8, no. 2 (April 1990), pp. 202–29.

10. U.S. General Accounting Office, *Employer-based Health Insurance: High Costs, Wide Variation Threaten System* (Washington, D.C.: September 1992), p. 32.

11. U.S. Department of Commerce, *Household Wealth and Asset Ownership: 1988: Survey of Income and Program Participation,* Series P-70, no. 22; Arthur Kennickell and Janice Shack-Marquez. "Changes in Family Finances from 1983 to 1989: Evidence from the Survey of Consumer Finances," *Federal Reserve Bulletin,* January 1992, pp. 1–18.

of health care costs over time would come much closer to some form of age-adjusted premiums than to pure community rating.[12]

This lifetime distribution argument paints too rosy a view of community rating, however. It looks only at one person's preferred distribution of health care expenses over an earning career; it does not examine the difference in burdens across the income categories of different lifetime earners. One earner (say, a banker) will have much less of a burden than another (say, a bank teller) over their respective lifetime earnings. And this analysis is simplistic in assuming that health risk is homogeneous for each age group. Clearly, different workers of the same age have widely varying health risks, even apart from the disabled who are covered by public funds. Community rating helps to equalize the burdens created by the variation in health status within an age group, but it does not compensate for the income differences among occupations. Community rating proposals usually address this equity dimension by requiring employees to pay only a portion of their insurance premiums, with some other mechanism for assisting employers of low-wage workers.

Personal Responsibility. The strongest argument against community rating is the unfairness of forcing others to pay for medical costs caused by voluntary lifestyle habits such as smoking, overeating, hang gliding, avoiding exercise, and not wearing seat belts.[13] Com-

---

12. For similar reasons, social policies that protect the elderly and burden the young are increasingly coming under attack as the aging of the baby-boom generation threatens to bankrupt funding mechanisms for social security and Medicare. See generally P. Johnson, C. Conrad, and D. Thompson, eds., *Workers versus Pensioners: Intergenerational Justice in an Aging World* (New York: St. Martin's Press, 1989); H. J. Aaron, B. P. Bosworth, and G. Burtless, *Can America Afford to Grow Old?* (Washington, D.C.: Brookings Institution, 1989); Phillip Longman, *Born to Pay: The New Politics of Aging in America* (Boston: Houghton-Mifflin, 1987)

13. There is a fascinating debate on whether these behaviors actually increase total *social* costs. One remarkable argument is that smoking does not cost society because those who suffer a premature death provide a windfall to pension funds and social security. Even medical expenses are in doubt, since everyone incurs them at some point, and, all things being equal, those who die early incur fewer in the aggregate. Robert L. Schwartz, "Making Patients Pay for Their Life-Style Choices," *Cambridge Quarterly of Healthcare Ethics*, vol. 4 (1992), pp. 393–400. These calculations fail to account, however, for the value of the lost life in terms either of psychic loss or of what the person could have contributed to the economy or to society. Moreover, they are not relevant to this inquiry, which is whether bad health habits increase insurance risk. Subsidiary windfalls to pension funds do not count in the

munity rating gives those who are irresponsible or risk seekers a free ride on the community's insurance pool.

This argument for risk rating is based on fairness, not necessarily on economic efficiency. The debate over whether cost savings will materially improve health habits has been surveyed above.[14] Employers increasingly believe that behavior is modifiable by either education or financial incentives, since many are creating health promotion programs that combine education with incentives or penalties to

---

health insurance calculus, nor do health care costs avoided by death.

The evidence is clear that bad health habits increase health insurance premiums. One study showed that annual claims costs of persons with bad health habits are eight times as high as those with good health habits. James Fries et al., "Reducing Health Care Costs by Reducing the Need and Demand for Medical Services," *New England Journal of Medicine*, vol. 329 (1993), pp. 321–25. See also J. Paul Leigh and James F. Fries, "Health Habits, Health Care Use and Costs in a Sample of Retirees," *Inquiry*, vol. 29 (Spring 1992), pp. 44–54 (smoking, heavy drinking, excess weight, failure to use seat belts, and low exercise are associated with $372–598 of direct costs per year); Roger Feldman, "Health Insurance in the United States: Is Market Failure Avoidable?" *Journal of Risk and Insurance*, vol. 54 (1987), pp. 298–313 ("according to one state insurance commissioner, 60–70 percent of all health insurance claims are for lifestyle-related illnesses"); W. G. Manning et al., *The Costs of Poor Health Habits* (Cambridge, Mass: Harvard University Press, 1991); Thomas A. Hodgson, "Cigarette Smoking and Lifetime Medical Expenditures," *Milbank Quarterly*, vol. 70 (1992), pp. 81–126 (health care expenditures over a lifetime increase with smoking and are as much as 47 percent higher for male heavy smokers).

14. See chapter 2, notes 17 and 18. In addition to efficiency in the form of improving health habits, Feldman and Dowd demonstrate that community rating threatens to undermine efficiency in the form of purchasing the optimal level of insurance. Charging a uniform rate for each subscriber assumes that each subscriber desires a uniform level of insurance. Because tastes for health insurance vary, a compromise will have to be reached in setting the level of insurance somewhere within the range of desired options. If a high end is chosen (one that high-risk subscribers are likely to prefer), low-risk subscribers will be forced to purchase more insurance than they want, creating excess moral hazard. If the uniform rate is set so as to produce a middle-range level of insurance, low-end subscribers still purchase too much while high-end subscribers receive too little. Any result, under this analysis, is imperfect compared with allowing unconstrained risk rating. Roger Feldman and Bryan E. Dowd, "Biased Selection—Fairness and Efficiency in Health Insurance Markets," in Helms, ed., *American Health Policy*, pp. 64–86.

decrease smoking, lose weight, increase exercise, and the like.[15] Even if these programs fail, however, opposition to pure community rating still has a strong ethical basis. Forcing those with conscientious health habits to pay the costs created by voluntary risky behavior violates norms of personal responsibility and moral blameworthiness.

This argument can be carried too far, however. Although it might tell us to step back from community rating, it does not justify full risk rating, nor does it tell us how to distinguish controllable from uncontrollable health risks and what our criterion of controllability should be.[16] Genetic disease is often cited as the quintessential uncontrollable health condition, but many conditions toward which we are genetically predisposed, such as cancer or heart disease, are triggered to some extent by controllable environmental influences. Moreover, even for a highly deterministic genetic disease such as hemophilia, it could be argued that the child's parents should pay because they chose to bring a defective newborn into existence. This callous argument shows that even controllable health risks may implicate privileged decisions that we would be loath to penalize. Should we pay more for not adhering to a strictly vegetarian diet, or for commuting long distances to work?[17]

Social versus Private Insurance. Some commentators attempt to resolve this myriad of competing fairness arguments by emphasizing the social character of health insurance.[18] When an insurance function is taken over by the government (socialized), variation in individual risk is usually not considered relevant to how the program is funded. Risk usually remains relevant only to how the program's benefits are distributed. Thus, for social insurance programs, such as disaster relief, disability income, and Medicaid, the funding comes from

---

15. Fries et al., "Reducing Health Care Costs by Reducing the Need and Demand for Medical Services," pp. 321–25; Marilyn J. Field and Harold T. Shapiro, eds., *Employment and Health Benefits: A Connection at Risk* (Washington, D.C.: Institute of Medicine; National Academy Press, 1993), p. 117.

16. For a lucid discussion of this issue in the context of income tax deductions, see Joel S. Newman, "The Deductibility of Nondiscretionary Personal Expenses," *American Journal of Tax Policy*, vol. 6 (1987), pp. 211–56.

17. For a forceful expression of these concerns, see Schwartz, "Making Patients Pay for Their Life-Style Choices."

18. Stone, "The Struggle for the Soul of Health Insurance," pp. 286–317; Norman Daniels, "Insurability and the HIV Epidemic," pp. 497–525; Donald W. Light, "The Practice and Ethics of Risk-Related Health Insurance," *Journal of the American Medical Association*, vol. 267, no. 18 (1992), pp. 2503–08.

broad-based tax revenues and is independent of each individual's potential claim on the fund. Precisely the opposite is true for private insurance, for which individual risk is the determinative criterion.[19]

A mandatory purchase system attempts to construct a hybrid. It uses private health insurance to help meet the social goal of universal coverage. In such a hybrid, is it more appropriate to say that a mandatory purchase requirement has socialized the private insurance industry or that the retention of private insurance has privatized the social program? Deborah Stone argues that private health insurance "operates on a deep contradiction" when it engages in risk rating by charging the most for insurance to those who need it most,[20] but this argument assumes that community rating is the norm for health insurance. Instead, the early existence of community rating can be seen as a fleeting historical anomaly that was out of keeping with all other forms of private insurance. According to this view, the deep contradiction is to require private insurers to ignore risk when the very business of insurance is to measure risk.

The point is that we do not yet have a consensus on whether the social or the private characterization applies. Since the characterization itself is being debated, it cannot be cited as the authority for how health insurance should be priced. Moreover, even if the social insurance description were accepted, the result would not necessarily be community rating. Some forms of social insurance are risk rated, and others employ a form of taxation that is much more progressive than community rating.[21] Compare, for instance, unemployment insurance premiums as a percentage of payroll, which is roughly proportionate to the risk insured, and Medicaid funding, which is a progressive and broad-based tax.

The redistributive characterization of community rating, however, depends on two assumptions, both of which are subject to challenge. First, it assumes that individuals have a property right to trade on their individual risk status. It can be argued, to the contrary,

---

19. Thomas Bodenheimer and Kevin Grumbach, "Financing Universal Health Insurance: Taxes, Premiums, and the Lessons of Social Insurance," *Journal of Health Politics, Policy and Law*, vol. 17, no. 3 (Fall 1992), pp. 439–62.

20. Stone, "The Struggle for the Soul of Health Insurance." The author overstates her argument when she argues that private insurers want to shun high risks entirely and that they make more money from low risks. Rather, insurers are pleased to sell to high-risk subscribers, and they may make even more money from them, so long as they can price their products accurately to reflect the risk. Witness Lloyds of London.

21. Bodenheimer and Grumbach, "Financing Universal Health Insurance."

that actuarial insurance risk is not an innate, personal endowment, such as one's intelligence, physical strength, or beauty, that one has an inherent right to exploit. One's risk status is a statistical construct that is formed only to the extent that acquiring individual risk information produces a cost-effective market advantage. Market-derived health risk is so capricious that it changes simply according to the job one holds, the area where one lives, or the risk profile of others who happen to hold the same job or select the same insurer.

The second assumption made by redistributive subsidy critics is that the alternative to mandatory community rating is a fully risk-rated market. To the contrary, most individuals already belong to a voluntary community-rated plan in the form of employee group rating. Although group insurance is usually described as experience rated, this is true only between groups. Within groups, a very strict version of community rating prevails in that employee contributions do not vary according to age or risk status, and often not even for differences in the type of insurance selected.

Community rating can be characterized as merely an attempt to bring to the deteriorating part of the market the same types of cross-subsidies that already prevail where the market works best—for large employee groups. This attempt to correct market failure can therefore be characterized as restructuring the market-derived source of one's risk status rather than as a forced redistribution from those who would most benefit from the complete unraveling of group insurance.

Requiring community rating does not, in and of itself, restructure the market to make insurers and subscribers oblivious to risk, however. Community rating is in such strong tension with the dynamics of the natural market because the market remains acutely sensitive to risk. Other market interventions discussed below, such as risk adjustment and risk-rated vouchers, might have this risk-desensitizing effect, but not community rating. Since risk differentials are real, the redistributive effect cannot be imagined away, especially if participation in a community-rated system is mandatory.[22] To

_____

22. So long as the purchase of community-rated insurance is voluntary, it can be said to impose no implicit taxation, since subscribers have the option of not participating in the pool. There are two levels of voluntariness: the one that prevailed historically with Blue Cross, where both community-rated and risk-rated insurance were available, and the one that prevails in New York, where all insurance is community rated at one end of the market, but market participation is not required. The argument based on voluntariness becomes much weaker if participation in community-rated pools is obtained by forcing nonsubscribers to go without a social necessity. Imagine the argument that the income tax is voluntary because one can choose not to work.

pretend that no cross-subsidy exists because the forced purchase of community-rated insurance redefines one's *a priori* risk status is like arguing that the prisoner who is allowed to pick his own cell has been set free. The point is more difficult to see for insurance only because of the intangible nature of risk.

On balance, there are compelling arguments from fairness on both sides of the community rating debate. Therefore, no social or political consensus is likely either to favor or to oppose pure community rating on equity grounds. This ethical stalemate suggests that compromises between pure community rating and unrestricted risk rating are plausible. It also suggests that, in striking a balance between risk pooling and risk segmenting, pragmatic concerns over administration should prevail.

The Feasibility of Community Rating

Biased Selection among Insurers. In chapter 3, we saw that community rating creates severe difficulties in a market of voluntary purchase by causing adverse selection against the market as a whole. In a mandatory system, however, no selection against the market can occur because everyone must purchase and thus contribute to the risk pool. Nevertheless, a different set of problems comes from biased selection—that is, both favorable and adverse selection or the uneven grouping of both good and bad risks.

It is sometimes said that community rating is essential to managed competition because it forces insurers to stop competing on the basis of how well they select risk.[23] Just the opposite is true. Community rating greatly intensifies insurers' incentives to engage in risk selection for the very reason that it precludes them from adjusting the premium to reflect individual risk. The need to control incentives for biased selection on the part of both insurers and subscribers creates formidable problems in administering a community-rated market.

Within a system of mandatory purchase, biased selection occurs among insurers in two forms: systemic and strategic. Systemic selection occurs because different insurers charge different rates according to their different communities of subscribers, causing subscribers to favor those with lower risk profiles. At the outset of community rating, some insurers will have lower risk profiles than others because of their past use of medical underwriting or because of random luck-

---

23. See, for example, "A Misleading Health Estimate," *New York Times*, November 3, 1993.

of-the-draw. Prices therefore will not perfectly reflect each insurer's efficiency in administrating insurance or in managing care. Competitive advantages gained by cost savings or service quality will be negated by these distorting effects on price, which will tend to undermine one of the purposes of a market-based system.

If those who switched insurers were of equal risk to those who stayed, these artificial price differences caused by historical or random distributions of risks would level out over time. Lower-risk insurers would attract new subscribers who represent a cross-section of the market, existing good and bad risks would regress to the mean, and the cards would be partially reshuffled for insurers who received a bad luck-of-the-draw in the past. For good reason, however, insurers fear that those who switch plans are healthier than average, particularly when they join managed-care plans. Patients who are sick are more attached to their doctors and therefore more reluctant to switch for a price advantage. Companies with an initial artificial price advantage, therefore, would build on the advantage each year as those who were only slightly behind at the outset fell further behind.[24] Eventually, insurers fear that the price disparity could force some of them out of business regardless of their inherent efficiency. Short of that extreme, these dynamics result in the market being less than optimally efficient.

Even if historical and accidental risk differentials are ironed out, a second form of biased selection occurs because good and bad risks do not sort themselves randomly among competing insurers. Instead, attributes of some insurers' plans attract healthier patients, and other attributes attract sicklier patients. Patients who make heavier use of their physicians are more hostile to the restrictions in choice of providers imposed by managed-care plans. Conversely, younger and healthier patients who have no physician ties and anticipate no need of medical services find these restrictions less objectionable. There is considerable debate, therefore, over whether fee-for-service plans systematically attract riskier patients than do HMOs.[25] Biased selection also occurs when unhealthy patients favor lower copayments than healthy patients do or when subscribers with mental illness gravitate toward plans that cover it.

Insurers can engage in countless techniques to encourage this

24. For an illustration of this progression, see U.S. Congress, House, Committee on Ways and Means, *Private Health Insurance: Options for Reform*, 101st Cong., 2d sess., September 20, 1990, p. 30.

25. See Charles William Wrightson, *HMO Rate Setting and Financial Strategy* (Ann Arbor: Health Administration Press, 1990), pp. 245–94.

strategic behavior to their benefit. Some are devious and improper, such as poor claims service for chronically ill patients and "field underwriting"—tacit encouragement of field agents to keep high-risk applications from reaching the home office. One HMO reportedly placed its enrollment office on the third floor of a building without an elevator. Other techniques are innocuous. Well-baby visits and an ample supply of pediatric specialties attract younger subscribers, and specialists in sports medicine attract healthy subscribers. Lesser coverage of prescription drugs discourages older patients, and deleting from an HMO's drug formulary expensive specialty drugs for rare conditions obviously deters subscribers suffering from those conditions. Simply choosing one advertising medium rather than another (fitness magazines rather than *Modern Maturity*) or marketing more aggressively in one part of town rather than another produces widely different combinations of age and health status. Similarly, a managed-care plan's attractiveness to different groups is strongly influenced by where it locates its treatment facilities and what kinds of doctors are in the network.

In sum, biased selection occurs both naturally, through patients' choices among different plans, and as a result of insurers' calculated use of covert selection devices. Moreover, opportunities for covert risk selection increase as health insurance moves toward managed care. Under the pure indemnity model with free choice of physician, insurance policies could be made more or less attractive only by varying their benefits. With managed care, the attractiveness of plans varies across a much wider spectrum, determined by the style of medical practice and the structure of the treatment network.

Some of these techniques can be controlled, but it is not possible or desirable to prohibit all avenues and motivations for selection.[26] For instance, requiring insurers to engage in marketing through purchasing cooperatives limits some abuses, but dictating the content of marketing may violate constitutionally protected speech.[27] Selec-

---

26. Even if a particular selection technique is prohibited, the prohibition is often ineffective or counterproductive because banning one technique simply forces insurers to shift to another that may be even more offensive. This occurred, for instance, with AIDS when some life insurers who were denied the right to test for the HIV virus began to refuse coverage based on stereotyped judgments of jobs and mannerisms that suggest a gay lifestyle.

27. The Supreme Court has consistently struck down states' efforts to ban advertising by professionals. Virginia State Board of Pharmacy v. Virginia Citizens Consumer Council, 425 U.S. 748 (1976) (finding a constitutional right to advertise prescription drug prices); Bates v. State Bar of Arizona, 433 U.S. 350 (1977) (upholding a constitutional right to advertise legal services). See

tion bias can also be reduced by reducing consumers' range of choice. Open enrollment, for instance, can be changed from once a year to every three years, except for relocation or a change in jobs. Other selection problems created by community rating might be eliminated by imposing a uniform benefits package, as is strongly urged by the Jackson Hole Group, one of the leading advocates for managed competition. However, these measures would sacrifice an important range of consumer choice and dampen competitive forces, which are the fundamental reasons for having a market system in the first place. Moreover, demand-side selection could not be eliminated without creating a uniform practice environment as well, since this too has a demonstrable effect on subscriber choice. The end point of this logic is to eliminate variety, experimentation, and choice for the sake of making a competitive process workable.

There are two alternative remedies for these selection problems that would avoid policing selection behavior so aggressively. The first would abandon or modify community rating, and the second would provide some behind-the-scenes adjustment. Allowing competing insurers some variation in their charges to reflect relative risks among different pools of patients alleviates selection problems by requiring subscribers to pay more of the actuarial value of their individual health risks. Increased risk rating encounters the objections surveyed above, however. Some persons have to pay more because of health and age factors beyond their control. Moreover, full risk rating cannot be allowed without reintroducing some of the evils of medical underwriting. Full risk rating would price insurance beyond the reach of some individuals and groups, and the underwriting process required to assess risks more accurately would add administrative overhead expense. Some compression in rate variation is therefore necessary, even though it creates biased selection problems.

The other remedy is to adopt a system of risk adjustment, which compensates insurers behind the scenes for their differential risk pools, in contrast to risk rating, which compensates them up front.

---

also Central Hudson Gas & Electric Corp. v. Public Service Commission, 447 U.S. 557 (1980), which strikes down the state ban on promotional advertising by electric utilities. The Court has sustained restrictions on the advertising of legal gambling, however, in Posadas de Puerto Rico Associates v. Tourism Company of Puerto Rico, 478 U.S. 328 (1986), and it has let stand a ban on the broadcast advertising of cigarettes. Capital Broadcasting Co. v. Mitchell, 333 F. Supp. 582 (D.C.D.C. 1971), affirmed without opin., 405 U.S. 1000 (1972). See also Red Lion Broadcasting Co. v. FCC, 395 U.S. 367 (1969), which allows broad regulation of the content of broadcasting, because of the scarcity of the airwaves and the need to limit access.

Risk adjustment aims to accomplish the same result as risk-rated premiums without passing risk differences on to individual consumers. If risk adjustment works well, insurers receive accurate compensation for individual risks and therefore have no incentive to attract better risks or discourage worse ones. This forces them to compete on the efficiency-enhancing attributes of their plans. And, if risk adjustment works well, premium differentials can be compressed or strict community rating enforced without oppressive burdens to high-risk subscribers and their insurers. Risk adjustment is therefore the magic potion for all that ails community rating. There is only one question: does it work?

The Mechanics of Risk Adjustment. Risk adjustment increases payments for higher-risk subscribers and lowers payments for lower-risk ones in proportion to the entire market's average risk. The math is tedious but fairly simple. Each subscriber is given a risk rating, which is averaged across each risk pool to determine the pool's total risk profile. If the average risk is set at 1, a subscriber projected to cost half the market's average would be rated 0.5; one projected to cost twice the average, 2.0. If these were the only two in the insurer's pool, the pool's risk profile would be 1.25. If there were only one other insurer in the market, its risk profile, by default, would be 0.75 times its size relative to the first, since risk adjustment is a zero-sum process. Assuming that both insurers in this example have the same number of subscribers, and assuming further that the average cost of insurance, less administrative overhead, is $3,000, then the lower-cost insurer would be required to transfer $1,500 ($3,000 x 0.25 x 2 subscribers) to the higher-cost insurer.

As a consequence, neither insurer would have an incentive to discourage unhealthy subscribers or to attract healthier ones. Moreover, if all insurers were equally efficient, all could charge the same community rate to their subscribers, regardless of their individual risks. A competitive market should approach this outcome. The contribution that the low-risk insurer makes will force it to raise its price from $2,250 to $3,000, while the risk-adjustment increment the high-risk insurer receives allows it to lower its rates from $3,750 to $3,000. If one insurer were more efficient, though, it could lower its community rate even further to attract more business. In other words, if risk adjustment works perfectly, the difference that subscribers see in community rates among competing insurers reflects the insurers' inherent efficiencies rather than the arbitrary clustering of risks among their subscriber pools.[28]

---

28. See generally Mark C. Hornbrook and Michael J. Goodman, "Adjusting Health Benefit Contributions to Reflect Risk," in Mark C. Hornbrook,

Transfer payments required by risk adjustment can be made in various ways. The simplest, now used in New York, requires each insurer rated lower than 1.0 to contribute to a central transfer pool and each insurer rated higher than 1.0 to draw from the transfer pool an amount proportionate to the insurer's risk profile and its number of subscribers. That is, at the $3,000 average, the contribution or withdrawal amount for each subscriber would be $15 for each hundredth of a point in the insurer's risk profile differential from 1. An alternative advocated by the economist Mark Pauly would provide each subscriber a risk-adjusted premium voucher to purchase a minimum set of health care benefits from any insurer. The insurer would then cash in the voucher from the government funding source for an amount proportionate to the subscriber's risk rating. A rough hybrid of these two approaches, which also contains an element of risk rating, has the employer pay the risk adjustment entirely as part of its share of the premium, so that the employee's share remains unaffected.

The most significant complication in risk-transfer payment occurs in setting the reference price for the market average. If all insurers offer identical coverage, this task is relatively simple. If insurers have different levels of coverage, however, risk can be calculated only in reference to a particular set of insurance benefits. Some proposals therefore require risk rating to be based on a standard set of minimum benefits that all insurers must offer. If insurers and subscribers want to contract for different benefits than the reference plan they can, but the cost differentials will not be reflected in the risk-adjustment process. In other words, they will bear the costs of the additional coverage with an unadjusted premium increment that reflects the enhanced benefits.

Whether this premium increment should be community rated is another topic of debate. Requiring the unadjusted premium increment to be community rated would invite unmonitored and uncorrected risk-selection tactics. Moreover, because supplemental insurance is voluntary and individually purchased, community rating may not be viable because of the severe adverse selection spiral that is likely to result from the disproportionate purchase by less healthy patients. If the premium increment were allowed to be risk rated, a more complex pricing structure would result in which the base premium reflecting the minimum benefits package would be commu-

ed., *Advances in Health Economics and Health Services Research: Risk-based Contributions to Private Health Insurance,* vol. 12 (Greenwich, Conn.: JAI Press 1991), pp. 41–76.

nity rated and risk adjusted, but the premium increment for benefits beyond the minimum package is fully risk rated. Another alternative would either require or allow insurers to offer more than one standard benefits package—for example, bare-bones, basic, standard, and Cadillac coverage—and then to adjust risk for each separately. This method increases the complexity of risk adjustment and may decrease its accuracy.

A second complication in calculating the reference price for market-wide risk adjustment is that some insurers manage the costs of care better than others. Therefore, the use of a single, average market price would penalize more efficient plans with lower risks and reward less efficient plans with higher risks. The more efficient plan would have to pay greater amounts into the transfer pool and the less efficient plan would be partially compensated for its inefficiency. Using a market average therefore dampens efficiency incentives. If the lowest cost plan in the market becomes the reference price, however, no one can be sure whether it reflects true efficiency rather than favorable risk selection. To resolve this impasse, plans must first be risk rated in reference to the market average and then rerated in reference to the lowest-cost risk-adjusted plan. Although this process is complex, the mechanisms of risk adjustment are more manageable than developing an actual risk-adjustment measure.

Techniques for Risk Adjustment. The most troublesome issue in risk adjustment is determining how to measure risk. The Clinton reform proposal is silent on techniques for risk adjustment. The same is true of every other major proposal for managed competition, including those of the Jackson Hole Group and of the Bush administration. Each of these delegates to experts the task of choosing the appropriate risk-adjustment measure. This deference to administrators implies that proven risk adjustors are in use and that determining the best one is merely a matter of technical expertise. In truth, this is hardly an accurate portrayal of the state-of-the-art in risk adjustment. Several adjustors are being developed, but they are all in early stages of testing and refinement, and each is plagued with flaws.

Because of the central importance of risk adjustment to managed competition, policy makers must have some acquaintance with the technical details of this complex and rapidly changing field. The ideal risk-adjustment technique would use an objective, easily detected, and reliable measure that gives as accurate and unbiased a prediction as possible of the variation in health care costs among different subscribers.[29] Death is a good predictor. Dead subscribers use no health care resources, death is not easily faked, and no one is likely to produce their own (or their subscribers') death in order to manipulate the measure. The only problem is that death predicts only one extreme end in the variation of health care costs.

More robust risk-adjustment systems in actual development or use can be categorized according to the basic measure of risk. The most straightforward predictor of future health care costs is past claims experience. Another simple measure uses a demographic profile that includes factors such as age, gender, and sometimes basic economic and social status such as employment and marital status. Greater sophistication and complexity are introduced by risk-adjustment systems that are based on diagnoses of the subscriber's medical condition and on kinds (not just cost) of recent treatment. Another category uses self-perceived health status (that is, asking subscribers how healthy they feel). These measures can be used singly or in different combinations.[30]

Claims experience and demographic factors such as age and sex are the risk-measurement tools in widest use by the insurance industry. However, they explain only a small part of the total variation in individual health care costs. The adjusted average per capita cost (AAPCC) method which is used by HCFA to pay Medicare HMOs, accounts for less than 1 percent of the variation in costs of treatment among individual Medicare beneficiaries by adjusting payment according to age, sex, welfare status, and institutional status.[31] As a result, the federal government lost rather than saved money on Medicare HMOs.[32]

Attempts to improve these demographic measures by including the individual's prior cost of treatment have had only modest success, increasing the proportion of variance explained to around 2 percent.[33]

29. See generally Richard V. Anderson, "Can Risk Assessment Tools Be Feasibly Used in the Health Benefit Marketplace?" in Hornbuck, *Advances in Health Economics and Health Services Research*, pp. 3–18.

30. See generally Mark C. Hornbrook and Michael J. Goodman, "Health Plan Case Mix: Definition, Measurement, and Use," in Hornbuck, *Advances in Health Economics and Health Services Research*, pp. 111–49.

31. Gerard F. Anderson et al., "Setting Payment Rates for Capitated Systems: A Comparison of Various Alternatives," *Inquiry*, vol. 27 (Fall 1990), pp. 225–33.

32. Robert Pear, "Medicare to Stop Pushing Patients to Enter H.M.O.'s," *New York Times*, December 27, 1993.

33. Mark C. Hornbrook, Michael L. Goodman, and Marjorie D. Bennett, "Assessing Health Plan Case Mix in Employed Populations: Ambulatory

This means that, if we measured the actual relationship (in a particular location and for a particular kind of coverage) between subscribers' past claims and their next year's expenses or between their age and sex and the next year's expenses and if we then adjusted the payments to community-rated insurance plans for each subscriber's characteristics, that adjustment would compensate insurers only for 1–2 percent of the variation in health care costs their subscribers are actually likely to experience. Most of the adjustment would therefore only add to the existing arbitrariness in risk distribution, either reducing or increasing the variation by random chance.

Measures of actual health status can be expected to perform considerably better depending on their sophistication. New York's risk-adjustment system combines demographic factors with selected high-cost diagnoses such as AIDS, diabetes, cancer, and vegetative state. However, a short list of high-cost treatments is a crude measure of risk that is unlikely to account for much of the total variation in treatment costs among subscribers. More comprehensive measures of health status create their own difficulties, however, resulting primarily from administrative problems and from bias.

The main problem in administration is collecting sufficient information. Some health-condition risk adjustors rely on episodes of inpatient hospitalization that can be collected from claims data. Claims data, however, give meager clinical information and may not exist at all within staff- and group-model HMOs. Better information can be garnered from medical records, but they are not computerized or systematized. The use of medical records also raises issues of confidentiality that are particularly sensitive in an employment-based insurance system that might give employers access to personal information. Moreover, a system based on past treatment leaves out anyone who has not been hospitalized in the relevant time frame. One attempt to correct this flaw relies on outpatient treatment, but this greatly amplifies the logistical problems of collecting data.

Health status measures for risk adjustment also create problems of bias and distortion. Consider, for instance, a measure that relies on recent medical treatment, which would encourage insurers to call in all subscribers for treatment just before measurement time. Consider instead a measure that looks at the patient's actual condition as indicated by diagnoses. As we know from the Medicare system that pays hospitals by diagnostic categories, diagnoses can also be manipulated. Moreover, adjusting for health status perversely

Morbidity and Prescribed Drug Models," in Hornbrook, *Advances in Health Economics and Health Services Research*, pp. 197–232.

rewards plans that provide inferior treatment. Similar concerns relate to treatment efficiency. If a health-status adjustment measure uses past treatment, and even if this measure is not manipulated, it still rewards plans that overtreat and penalizes those that are more economical. These flaws undermine the ability of a competitive market system to reward efficiency in the management of health care.[34]

Conscious of these problems, the developers of health-status measures for risk adjustment attempt to avoid them. They search for the most accessible and reliable sources of data, and they restrict their inquiry to diagnoses and treatments least subject to discretionary judgment or manipulation. In doing so, however, they sacrifice some accuracy by forgoing valuable information. As a consequence, these measures have shown only limited success. The best measures predict less than 10 percent of the variation among individual health care costs over a year.[35]

The final category of risk adjustors—self-perceived health status—is intriguing because it proves almost as predictive as the other adjustors, despite its apparent subjectivity.[36] Researchers at RAND have devised a thirty-six–item questionnaire that inquires into subjects' general sense of physical and mental well-being, with

34. An additional source of bias arises from the manner in which a health risk measure is developed and tested. The process is to assign scores to patients from a representative population, whose use of health care resources is observed over an ensuing period. Weights are assigned to each score according to these results and then applied to a similar test population to see how accurately they predict that population's use of resources. The bias springs from the particular population and treatment setting used. Elderly Medicare patients distort the ability of risk adjustors to predict health care costs across all age groups. Similarly, other adjustors have been tested primarily in HMO treatment settings or primarily in one location of the country. Testing a measure as broadly as possible does not solve this problem, since a risk adjustor should reflect some characteristics of a particular region or patient population. Local calibration of risk adjustors may, however, impose an inordinate burden on their development.

35. The literature is summarized and discussed in White House Task Force on Health Risk Pooling, *Health Risk Pooling for Small-Group Health Insurance* (January 1993); Gerard F. Anderson et al., "Setting Payment Rates for Capitated Systems: A Comparison of Various Alternatives," *Inquiry*, vol. 27 (Fall 1990), pp. 225–33; and Hornbrook and Goodman, "Health Plan Case Mix," in Hornbrook, *Advances in Health Economics and Health Services Research*, pp. 111–49.

36. Mark C. Hornbrook and Michael J. Goodman, "Assessing Relative Health Plan Risk with the RAND36 Health Survey," unpublished manuscript (1993).

questions such as "Do you feel tired?" or "How much pain have you had lately?" rather than "What illnesses have you had?" People who feel unhealthy are expected to seek medical care, whether or not they are actually doing well. Because this measure does not depend on whether one has used the health care system or has been covered, it avoids biases and opportunities for manipulation that can arise when data come from health care providers and insurers rather than directly from subscribers. However, self-perceived health status is subject to other sources of bias that might be more disturbing. Some social classes and ethnic groups, for example, may overreport or underreport their ailments according to the degree of stoicism or hypochondria that prevails in their community. To correct for such bias, membership in the relevant classes may be included as an additional adjustment.

The risk-adjustment effort should not be doomed by these imperfections, but the complex process of developing and testing a good health cost predictor is still in an early stage. Although no proven risk adjustor is ready to be put into full-scale use, the development of health risk adjustors is certainly worth pursing if there is some prospect that a workable measure will emerge. That prospect hinges on how much variation in health care costs must be explained for managed competition to function smoothly. The 5 to 8 percent explanation of variation currently achieved by health status measures may seem small in isolation, but this perception changes in view of the total possible explainable variation. The degree of variation explained also depends on whether it is measured at the level of a large group or at an individual level.

If individual variation were fully explainable, no one would have an incentive to purchase insurance; they would instead consult a statistician to learn how much money to set aside for future loss. Perfect risk adjustment would be tantamount to cost-based reimbursement since it would pay insurers exactly what it cost to treat each subscriber. Rather than ask what percentage of total variation health adjustment measures explain, we should judge them according to the portion of *explainable* variation they account for.

According to rough estimates, it is theoretically possible to predict only 15–20 percent of the individual variation in health care costs. The rest of variation is due to true randomness.[37] In this light,

---

37. See J. Newhouse, W. G. Manning, E. B. Keeler, and E. M. Sloss, "Adjusting Capitation Rates Using Objective Health Measures and Prior Utilization," *Health Care Financing Review*, vol. 10, no. 3 (Spring 1989), pp. 41–53.

the 5–8 percent that has been achieved looks much better and restores our confidence in the ultimate success of this venture.

Moreover, variation of any sort, health care costs included, is much wider and much less subject to statistical explanation at an individual than at a group level. This is the core insight from the law of large numbers, which is at the foundation of insurance. The percentage of variation explained increases dramatically when these risk-adjustment measures are applied to group variation, that is, differences in cost between groups rather than between individuals within a group. Depending on the size of the group (from 50 to more than 1,000), the variation explained increases to well over 50 percent for the various risk adjustors that have been tested.[38]

The critical question for risk adjustors then becomes which test—individual or group prediction—is more appropriate. The answer depends on refining our sense of why risk adjustment is important. One goal is to level the uneven distribution of risks among competing insurers so that their community-rated premiums better reflect comparative efficiencies in managing care and administering the insurance function.

To serve this function, risk must be predicted only at the level of each insurer's total pool. Under managed competition as proposed by President Clinton and others, insurers' risk pools can be expected to be quite large, since one goal of these plans is to reduce the number of competing insurers in each area. Insurers will be allowed to form separate risk pools only for a limited number of different insurance products (such as HMOs versus fee-for-service plans, and basic versus standard coverage). At this large-group level, even rough risk adjustors such as age and prior claims should suffice.

A second purpose of risk adjustment, however, is to remove the incentive for insurers to engage in risk selection. Making good and bad risks equally attractive to insurers forces them to compete on the basis of their product rather than their skills at risk selection. This purpose is advanced only if risk prediction is accurate at the level at which insurers solicit business. Purchasing cooperatives require insurers to compete at the margin for individual subscribers, since their purpose is to offer employees of both small- and large-employer groups a choice among insurance plans. Risk adjustment must therefore be accurate at an individual level to counteract incentives for risk selection.

---

38. See Stephen T. Hayes, "Demographic Risk Factors Derived from HMO Data," in Hornbrook, *Advances in Health Economics and Health Services Research*, pp,. 17–196.

But how accurate? Since the present purpose is to counteract intentional risk-selection, perfect risk prediction is not necessary. A risk adjustor need be only as accurate at risk selection as insurers themselves are. In the past, insurers have relied on imprecise measures, such as claims experience or demographics, so the task seems all too easy. Mark Pauly argues, for instance, that a risk adjustor need detect only the 5–15 percent of applicants who are typically turned down for coverage or offered substandard rates.[39] The solution will not be so simple, however, under the new market system created by managed-competition reform.

Managed competition increases both the incentives and the opportunities for risk selection. The incentives to screen for individual risk are heightened the more that rate variation is compressed. The opportunities to engage in covert selection are increased by the movement from traditional indemnity insurance to managed-care plans (because of the control over the treatment environment). Market reform will control some forms of individual risk selection by mandating uniform benefits packages and controlling marketing activities, but it cannot control all forms.

Finally, even if academic researchers are convinced that they can explain individual variation as well as insurers, risk adjustors will not accomplish their goal unless insurance underwriters are convinced. Since underwriters rely on a variety of both subjective and objective risk indicators (including pure intuition)—indicators that are not the same as the risk-adjustment measure—they are likely to believe (even if it is not true) that they can outmaneuver a risk-adjustment system. As Deborah Stone has observed, the techniques of risk assessment and underwriting "are so deeply embedded in the structure and mentality of insurance employees that they will be hard to eradicate. . . . Billions of dollars, millions of jobs, and innumerable organizations depend on the underwriting function," which will continue despite market reform for the life and disability insurance business that most large health insurers maintain.[40]

---

39. Mark Pauly, "Killing with Kindness: Why Some Forms of Managed Competition Might Needlessly Stifle Competitive Managed Care," in Robert B. Helms, ed., *Health Policy Reform: Competition and Controls* (Washington, D.C.: AEI Press, 1993).

40. Stone, "The Struggle for the Soul of Health Insurance," p. 313. Moreover, as Joseph Newhouse demonstrates, the relationship between variance explained and diminished incentive to select risk is nonlinear, such that explaining 70 percent of risk reduces by less than half the profits that insurers can make from risk selection. Therefore, it may be necessary to explain virtually all variance in order to substantially eliminate biased selec-

None of this means that adequate prediction of individual variation is unachievable, only that the task will require continued vigi-
lance. Confidence in risk adjustment will come only from real-
world experience.

Retrospective Risk Adjustment and Reinsurance. A final salvation
for risk adjustment is to conduct it on a retrospective rather than a
prospective basis. Retrospective risk adjustment has two meanings.
One is to apply a prospective measure several times a year to detect
as much of a particular risk indicator as possible. Using age as an
adjustor, for instance, one could tote up the age profile once a month
rather than once a year to capture changes that occur as the result of
disenrollments and new enrollments.[41] Similarly, for health status,
one could measure patients' diagnoses and perceived health status
more frequently than once a year. Midyear measures do not alter the
prospective nature of the risk measure; they simply shorten the time
over which risk is predicted.

Another method of retrospective risk adjustment is to monitor
throughout the year the actual costs of patient treatment and to adjust
premium payments accordingly. This is a fundamentally different
operation since it measures exactly what prospective risk adjustment
attempts to predict. One component of New York's risk-adjustment
system, for instance, is to pay insurers a scheduled amount for each
subscriber who actually receives treatment from a high-cost list,
which includes organ transplants and cancer treatment. This purely
retrospective means of adjustment shifts the insurance function for
the listed costs from the individual insurer to the central risk-transfer
pool. It therefore constitutes a stop-loss form of reinsurance.

Applied to discrete categories of cases, retrospective risk adjustment can be a useful backstop for the worst failings of prospective
risk-adjustment measures, much as outlier payments under Medicare
DRGs correct for that system's largest inaccuracies. If applied across-
the-board, however, this form of adjustment would render the insurance function meaningless, since insurers would then bear no risk
for any of their costs. Naturally, this is not proposed, but it demon-

---

tion. Joseph P. Newhouse, "Patients at Risk: Health Reform and Risk Adjustment," *Health Affairs*, vol. 13., no. 1 (Spring 1994), pp. 132–46.

41. Another approach is to reconcile at the end of the year the errors that
occurred in the initial projection of the insurer's annual risk profile. This
"truing up" is equivalent to the manner in which Medicare makes yearend
adjustments to its periodic interim payments under the DRG system to
account for the actual number of patients admitted and their actual diagnoses.

strates the danger in retrospective adjustors, namely, that they remove from the insurer the incentive to control the costs of care, and they do so for the very cases that cost the most. This also shifts insurance risk on the entity that funds the transfer pool, which, if it were a government entity, would constitute a single-payer system with private insurers serving only a claims-processing function.

Retrospective risk adjustors should therefore be used sparingly and in a manner that retains some incentive for cost control. The policy staff that developed the Bush administration's reform plan suggested that retrospective risk adjustment be used as a transitional measure until more accurate and better tested prospective adjustors are developed.[42] Joseph Newhouse proposes as a permanent solution a partial capitation rate that blends capitation with fee-for-service or cost-based reimbursement. By adjusting the blend, a proper combination of cost-containing and risk-accepting incentives can be maintained across the spectrum of treatment costs.[43]

By referring to reinsurance, we have come full circle, back to components of insurance market reform that are proposed under a system of voluntary purchase. This intersection in the analysis demonstrates that prospective reinsurance is itself a form of risk adjustment—one available to insurers on a self-help basis. The prospective reinsurance mechanism advocated by commercial insurers adjusts for uneven distribution of risk, and it neutralizes the incentive to select against bad risks by allowing insurers to pass their high-risk groups and individuals to a central pool. The advantage of reinsurance over an administered risk-adjustment system is that reinsurance allows insurers to identify their own high-risk cases. This avoids the need for academic researchers and government administrators to outguess the industry's underwriters. In addition, since the predictable losses by the reinsured pool are made up by assessments (usually against insurers themselves), reinsurance makes more explicit the internal subsidies built into a community-rated system.[44]

This hands-off form of risk adjustment is not a perfect one, however, for reasons surveyed in chapter 3. First, the reinsurance decision itself is a form of risk selection and so would reward insurers for their selection skills. Second, reinsurance operates only above the selection threshold established by the reinsurance premium, leaving

---

42. White House Task Force on Health Risk Pooling, Health Risk Pooling for Small-Group Health Insurance (January 1993).

43. Newhouse, "Patients at Risk."

44. Gene Steuerle makes this point in "Community Rating of Health: How Much Is Appropriate?" *Tax Notes*, May 31, 1993, p. 1269.

selection incentives below that threshold unaffected. Third, reinsurance was designed for, and works best with, whole groups rather than individuals, but under managed competition, selection incentives would operate at an individual subscriber level. Finally, reinsurance lowers or eliminates insurers' incentives to monitor the costs of care.

Reinsurance is particularly unsuited for community rating because it applies only to high-risk cases; therefore, it does not neutralize the incentive to select lower risks. Reinsurance works better under a system that allows some flexibility in risk rating. Community rating allows insurers to profit from low-risk cases, whereas in a system that allows some rate variation, market forces drive down premiums for low-risk subscribers. Risk adjustment is not necessary at the low end of the range unless low risks fall below the rating bands, but lower rates tend to stay within a reasonable range of the market average because no person is so healthy as to have no expenses. Put another way, enough people are healthy that no one stands out as extremely healthy.[45] The same is not true for unhealthy people. Their insurance risk is so high that some rate compression is necessary, and a reinsurance mechanism is needed to distribute fairly the resulting burden of taking on high-risk subscribers. Therefore, even though reinsurance does not fit well with pure community rating, it may be a sensible alternative in a market that allows some variation in rates, an alternative that is preferable to the administrative problems created by regulatory risk adjustment.

In contrast, the complexities of selection bias, risk adjustment, and reinsurance that are created by rate compression may make it not worth the effort. This is the conclusion drawn by health economist Mark Pauly, who vigorously defends mandatory purchase in a fully risk-rated market. Pauly points to the data cited earlier[46] indicating that only a small percentage of the population is subject to substandard rates. For this portion, Pauly would distribute individual subsidies to make insurance affordable rather than craft an elaborate scheme for controlling the risk selection that results from the hidden

---

45. This fact is illustrated by the concentration of health care expenditures among a small number of users. In any given year, 5 percent of a group will account for almost 60 percent of expenditures, while the bottom 70 percent of the group uses less than 10 percent of the total expenditures. M. Berk and Alan Monheit, "The Concentration of Health Care Expenditures: An Update," *Health Affairs* (Winter 1992), pp. 145–49 (national figures, based on NMES 1987 data).

46. See chapter 3, notes 38–40.

and regressive subsidies implicit in community rating.[47] Pauly's proposal will require a subsidy methodology that is both complicated and expensive, particularly since he calls for an individual rather than an employer mandate. Moreover, his proposal is convincing only if risk variation based on age and location is acceptable. Because these factors can combine to produce premium differentials of five fold or more, a fully risk-rated system will require subsidies for even those of average health.

Purchasing Cooperatives

The core feature of all proposals for managed competition reform—Democratic, Republican, and academic—is their reliance on purchasing cooperatives for the marketing and selection of insurance. This superficial consensus masks deep underlying divisions on how these cooperatives would be structured and run. Chapter 3 discusses the advantages of purchasing cooperatives and analyzes several design issues that relate primarily to their use in a system of voluntary insurance purchase. Following is a summary of the areas of disagreement about the design of purchasing cooperatives that relate to both voluntary and mandatory systems.[48]

Passive versus Aggressive. The most divisive issue relating to purchasing cooperatives is whether they should act as passive price takers or aggressive negotiators. The argument for aggressive negotiation is that individuals and small groups lack the bargaining clout of large employers to press hard for price reduction. Larger groups therefore enjoy deep discounts that insurers or providers allegedly compensate for by shifting costs to smaller purchasers. One purpose of a purchasing cooperative, then, is to aggregate and exercise purchasing power by contracting with only a limited number of insurers in each market based on competitive bids.

---

47. Pauly, "Killing with Kindness."
48. This discussion draws heavily from Elliot K. Wicks, Richard E. Curtis, and Kevin Haugh, "The ABCs of HIPCs," *Journal of American Health Policy*, vol. 3, no. 2 (March/April 1993), pp. 29–34; and from Elliot K. Wicks, "Aggressive Regulator or Passive Price-Taker: What Role Should HIPCs Play?" *Journal of American Health Policy*, vol. 3, no. 4 (July/August 1993), pp. 21–25. See also Henry N. Butler, *Unhealthy Alliances: Bureaucrats, Interest Groups, and Politicians in Health Reform* (Washington, D.C.: AEI Press, 1994); Clark C. Havinghurst, *Remaking Health Alliances* (Washington, D.C.: AEI Press, 1994).

The most legitimate[49] public policy concerns raised by this approach are that purchasing cooperatives may wield too much economic power and that they may select among insurers according to the wrong criteria. If cooperatives acquire too much power, they may begin to act more like market regulators than market competitors. Arizona's Medicaid program, the Arizona Health Care Cost Containment System, provides an illustration. AHCCCS was designed to use competitive bidding to select among the lowest-cost HMO-style insurance plans in each of the state's markets. The competitive bids, however, were consistently higher than the AHCCCS budget would allow. As the bidding process has evolved, AHCCCS announces in advance the per capita price it is willing to pay and individual plans elect whether to submit bids. In other words, a system designed as the epitome of a competitive insurance market has become a purely price-regulated market. The same could easily happen for large, monopsonistic purchasing cooperatives.

At the furthest extreme, aggressive cooperatives might declare a total market failure and take over the insurance function by contracting directly with providers on behalf of member subscribers. If participation in such risk-bearing cooperatives were mandatory, the cooperatives would evolve into a single-payer system indistinguishable from national health insurance. To avoid this outcome, the Clinton proposal prohibits cooperatives from assuming any risk-bearing function.

Short of nationalizing health insurance, aggressive cooperatives may create an overly price-sensitive market by selecting among insurers primarily because of price, to the detriment of subscribers willing to pay more for better service. If purchasing cooperatives set quality requirements, however, they simply impose another form of regulation. Competitive forces would be allowed to determine quality only within the price and service range that the cooperative makes available to subscribers. Opponents of aggressive cooperatives are concerned that this range would be far too narrow, both at the low-quality and the high-quality ends. Instead, these opponents argue, purchasing cooperatives should play the highly passive role of market

---

49. A less legitimate concern is that selective contracting will lead to consolidation of the insurance industry, with only a handful of large insurers left in each market after smaller insurers that lack the capital to form extensive provider networks have been driven out of business. There is no public policy reason to favor smaller insurers over larger ones, or more insurers over fewer, provided that a sufficient number remain to maintain competitive market conditions.

facilitator that accepts all insurers that meet truly minimum standards, leaving to individual consumer choice which insurers will flourish and which will be driven out of the market.

Concerns over aggressive cooperatives can easily be exaggerated, however. These concerns might also be motivated more by parochial forms of industry self-interest than by the public policy arguments that have been articulated. The present lack of bargaining power is a real problem for individuals and small to medium-sized employers. Passive cooperatives will not solve this problem. In addition, multiplying the number of insurers greatly increases the biased selection problems discussed above. Concerns over cooperatives gaining too much power or playing a regulatory role can be addressed by limiting the cooperatives' scope, by forcing them to compete among themselves, or by altering their governance structure.

Closed versus Open. A system of managed competition must decide the proper scope of purchasing cooperatives. Analysts agree that cooperatives are appropriate for individual and small-group purchasers, and most agree that employers should be allowed to opt out when they grow to a certain size. There is disagreement on where the line between small and large should be drawn and whether large employers above the line should be allowed to opt in.

The best way to avoid the selection problems discussed in chapter 3 is for participation in purchasing cooperatives to be mandatory for a certain segment of the market, although an optional participation system could exist even in a market that requires everyone to obtain insurance somewhere. Cooperatives need not cover the entire market. Large employers have solid grounds for opposing mandatory participation since their end of the market already operates like a successful purchasing cooperative system. These employers can simply be declared "corporate alliances," as the Clinton plan does.

One way to determine the size of the groups that are required to participate is to look at the portion of the market that is not functioning well on its own. Usually, this results in drawing the line at around 100. Even groups of this size, however, have much to gain from the purchasing clout and economies of scale created by cooperatives, as demonstrated in figure 2–1 (found in chapter 2). Larger groups may also gain from the expanded range of choice in cooperatives, since even employers of several thousand often select only one or two insurers. The dominant motivation for large cooperatives is the social and political objective of establishing a broader base over which to spread the higher costs of insuring nonworkers. It has been estimated under the Clinton proposal, for example, that employers' community rate is increased 14 percent by including these higher-risk groups in the pool, and this is with the employer cutoff at 5,000.[50] Obviously, the hidden subsidy would be unacceptable if the employer base shrank to the level of 100 proposed by others.

Once the line is drawn, we must determine whether it is exclusive as well as inclusive. In other words, conceding that groups below this level cannot opt out, can groups above it opt in? The argument in favor is that efficiencies and expanded choice might be gained even by larger groups. Allowing any form of choice, however, will create a selection bias. Some larger employers will opt in because they find the community-rated premiums of a cooperative more attractive than the experience-based rate they would be required to pay for an aging workforce. To avoid attracting only high-risk large groups, purchasing cooperatives would have to charge a risk-adjusted premium to employers that opt in. A basic risk adjustor such as age may suffice for large groups.

Multiple versus Monopolistic. Yet another divisive issue is whether there should be a single cooperative for each area rather than overlapping, competing cooperatives. Several arguments support allowing employers or individuals to choose among competing cooperatives. First, such choice would reduce concern over monopsony power and market exclusion. Second, it would allow rivalry among cooperatives, which creates an incentive for them to perform well. A critical concern about cooperatives is that they have no obvious impetus to act aggressively in the interests of consumers and to resist industry capture. Although various governing structures, discussed below, address this concern, experience with government agencies and with some Blue Cross plans suggest caution nevertheless about locating so much regulatory and economic power in a single entity. Third, many successful cooperatives are already run by business groups, chambers of commerce, and government employers. It would be ironic for managed-competition reform to destroy the precursors to the purchasing cooperative concept that gave birth to this reform.

---

50. *Business and Health,* January 1994, p. 12, reporting on Lewin-VHI estimates. Similar cross-subsidies are created by the manner in which cooperative boundaries are drawn between rural and urban areas and between socioeconomic and racial groups that contribute greater or lesser costs to the community-rated pool. This is why James F. Blumstein has observed that the effect of large cooperatives is to institutionalize cost shifting, not to avoid cost shifting, as is sometimes argued. See Blumstein, "Health Care Reform: The Policy Context," *Wake Forest Law Review,* vol. 29 (1994), pp. 15–46.

Nevertheless, competing cooperatives would create a range of additional problems. Would each insurer be allowed to contract with only one cooperative, or could it do business with all of them? If the latter, would the insurer have to offer the same price in each cooperative? If the former, would it be feasible to allow exclusive contracting between cooperatives and insurers in markets dominated by a single large insurer such as Blue Cross? Similarly, could employers select only one cooperative or several? If only one, what effect does this have in local markets dominated by a single employer?

In addition, multiple cooperatives would create selection problems that would complicate the risk-adjustment process. Would there be a single risk-adjustment mechanism across the market or only within each cooperative? If the latter, then would it also be necessary to adjust among cooperatives? As with every other dimension of insurance market reform, each step toward creating a better functioning market cascades into numerous compounding complexities. The only obvious way to solve these difficulties would be to create another authority to oversee the multiple-cooperative structure, which would merely elevate the debate to yet another tier. At some point, it becomes necessary to live with imperfection.

Private versus Public. A final concern is the governing structure of a purchasing cooperative. Walter Zelman, an architect of California Insurance Commissioner John Garamendi's influential managed-care plan and a Clinton adviser, outlines a range of possibilities from purely governmental to purely private.[51] As a governmental entity, a cooperative could be run like a state health department or a consumer protection agency, with appointed or elected officials who exercise state or federal regulatory powers. This structure would have the broadest possible public accountability, but it would be constrained by requirements of constitutional due process and of administrative procedures that limit government actions.

At the other extreme, the cooperative could be a purely private entity under contract with a government agency. Much of the day-to-day management of Medicare is conducted by private, for-profit insurance companies and physician groups in the form of fiscal intermediaries and peer review organizations. This model lacks any assurance that the cooperative would represent the proper interests. The only direct oversight mechanism in the private-contractor model

---

51. Walter A. Zelman, "Who Should Govern the Purchasing Cooperative?" *Health Affairs*, vol. 12, supp. (1993), pp. 49–57.

is the contract performance specifications imposed by the governmental overseer.

A public corporation is a hybrid model used by many utility companies. These nominally private entities are created by state charters (or statutes) specifying a unique governance structure designed to give the entity public accountability. For utility companies, this structure typically entails a board composed entirely or with a large majority of consumers. For a purchasing cooperative, the board would be composed of purchasers—both employers and ordinary subscribers. This is the model favored by the Clinton proposal, which strictly limits participation in governance by any person connected with the provider or insurer communities. The interests of these communities are represented only through advisory committees.

Which structure is most appropriate depends in large measure on the intended function of the cooperative. The more regulatory the role of the cooperative, the more governmental it should be and the broader its base of accountability. The structure of a purely private entity would be most appropriate for a system of voluntary cooperatives or voluntary participation. The structure of a government agency would be more in keeping with a cooperative that exercises rate regulatory functions and controls market entry and exit.

A hybrid, public corporation model seems well suited to the combined functions that many managed competition advocates envision. They see cooperatives acting as aggressive negotiators and market managers, yet functioning within a predominantly private marketplace. Limiting board composition to purchasers in the cooperative is in keeping with the cooperative's primary function as a purchasing agent. If cooperatives have more overt regulatory powers over providers and insurers, however, it becomes more difficult to defend the exclusion of these groups from the governance structure and from the decision process used to impose regulation. Basic democratic principles argue against cooperatives having it both ways: privatizing to the extent necessary to avoid requirements of due process, yet possessing quasi-regulatory powers without including all affected groups in the cooperative's governance structure.

5
Conclusion

Although this book has refrained from prescriptive solutions to the health care crisis, this analysis would be incomplete without drawing some conclusions. The following summary consists of the major points made in each portion of this book.

1. Both the social benefits of private insurance and its internal logic must be respected in any attempt to rehabilitate the market for private health insurance. Private insurers should not be given a role that they are incapable of assuming nor should the benefits of a private market mechanism be eroded in the process of market reform. Primarily, this requires that some degree of risk rating should be retained. Risk assessment is fundamental to the functioning of private insurance, and it provides social benefits by creating incentives for risk reduction. Controlling the excesses of risk rating does not require its elimination.

Conversely, it is plausible to introduce some cross-subsidy in the pricing of private health insurance. Insurers must recognize the larger social function that health insurance has assumed as the primary vehicle for financing universal access to health care. More explicit forms of subsidization than rate compression and guaranteed issue might be desirable in theory, but government has rarely succeeded in crafting an unobjectionable redistributive program.

2. The proposals for reforming the small-group market, though complex and industry-driven, for the most part are sensible and have been well received in the states where they were first enacted. Their limited ambition must be kept in mind, however. Guaranteed issue, insurance portability, rate compression, reinsurance, purchasing co-operatives, and elimination of some mandated benefits are intended to help those who want insurance but have been unable to buy it. These reforms will make insurance more expensive for many who have purchased insurance before and so cause some to drop coverage. Those who are hurt modestly will far outnumber those who are helped greatly. Therefore, we can have no confidence that these reforms will advance us toward the twin goals of universal access and cost containment. At best, they will do little more than stabilize the

private market and protect it from further deterioration.

3. Because of adverse selection, pure community rating creates severe feasibility problems in a market of voluntary purchase, particularly for individuals and small groups. Community rating can function better with mandatory purchase, but biased selection among insurers tends to create pricing distortions that undermine the purpose of a market mechanism and that may unfairly drive some insurance companies out of business. Moreover, problems of biased selection may make it difficult or impossible to offer insurance that is more generous than the standard package, which would effectively mandate a single-tier system. A workable risk-adjustment mechanism is therefore essential to community rating. The difficulty is that such mechanisms are still early in their development and are plagued with problems of accuracy, distortion, and administration.

4. Purchasing cooperatives, though attractive in conception, raise a host of new complications. They can serve any number of different functions in markets of both voluntary and mandatory purchase, which gives rise to disputes over their scope, powers, and governance. Most of these disputes turn on the fundamental question of how regulatory or market driven the purchase and delivery of health insurance should be. In the new realm of managed competition, the battle over whether management or competition is to have the upper hand is only now being waged.

Glossary

Adverse selection. The market distortion that arises when subscribers have more knowledge about their individual risks than insurers have or that insurers are allowed to reflect in their premiums. The effect is that, when insurance purchase is voluntary, a disproportionate number of high-risk subscribers will enroll. Adverse selection, if severe enough, can set into motion a price spiral that can cripple or destroy an insurance market. An insurer must increase its premium to anticipate adverse selection, forcing lower-risk subscribers to opt out, which pushes the price even higher, causing even more good risks to drop out. Opting not to purchase at all is adverse selection against the market as a whole. Opting to purchase from one insurer rather than another is adverse selection within the market, which is also known as *biased selection*.

Biased selection. The market imperfection that results from the uneven grouping of risks among competing subscribers. Biased selection includes favorable selection (attracting good risks and repelling bad ones) as well as *adverse selection* (which is the reverse). Biased selection can occur naturally, according to historical or accidental patterns, or it can occur strategically, according to conscious choices by either subscribers or insurers. Insurers' strategic efforts to gain favorable selection are known as risk selection, which is discussed under *medical underwriting*.

Blocks of business. Insurers traditionally categorize their products in blocks (or books or classes) of business, according to the basic type of policy and the way in which it is marketed. Thus, a health insurer might maintain separate blocks for its individual policies, its small-group policies, its HMO business, and insurance sold to trade associations.

Community rating. A method whereby an insurer charges each subscriber the same price in a given location, regardless of the subscriber's perceived health risk. Pure community rating allows the price to vary only according to the type of insurance and to family composition. Adjusted community rating allows separate prices based on age categories. Group rating allows the price to vary from one group to the next based on each group's prior claims experience.

ERISA (Employee Retirement Income Security Act of 1974). A federal law that primarily regulates pension funds but that has the secondary effect of preempting state law as it applies to other employee benefits, such as health insurance. A "savings clause" in ERISA allows states to regulate insurance, but federal courts have narrowly interpreted what is allowable insurance regulation. Also, a "deemer clause" declares that self-insured employers shall not be deemed to be insurers for purpose of state regulation. The net effect is that all employer-provided health insurance is immune from state contract or tort law, and that states may not regulate in any manner the health benefits offered by self-insured employers.

Guaranteed issue. An element of small-group market reform that precludes insurers from turning down any subscriber. Also known as open enrollment. A related component is guaranteed renewability of insurance, which prevents dropping any subscriber except for fraud or nonpayment.

Law of large numbers. The statistical phenomenon that the secondary risk known as *variance* is reduced as a larger number of similar primary risks are grouped. To illustrate, the odds that a series of coin tosses will produce exactly 50 percent heads is increased the more times the coin is tossed. This reduction in secondary risk is the primary reason that insurance exists.

Managed care. The general set of techniques used to coordinate the process and control the costs of medical care. Specific techniques include requiring patients to seek care from selected doctors and hospitals, rewarding physicians for economizing decisions, and requiring doctors to receive authorization before starting expensive treatment. Managed-care organizations include health maintenance organizations, individual practice associations, and preferred provider organizations.

Managed competition. An approach to health care reform that presents individual subscribers with a range of enrollment options among private health plans in an environment that manages the selection process and that makes individuals pay for the differences in price among the insurance options they choose. Usually, managed competition is applied to a mandatory purchase reform plan, but it can also operate in a voluntary market.

Medical underwriting. The general process of assessing individual subscribers for medical risk and making business decisions about whom to cover and how much to charge. Also known as risk selection or risk assessment. Specific techniques include redlining (refusing to sell in certain areas), blacklisting (refusing to sell to certain industries), churning or low-balling (charging unrealistically low rates at first and later canceling or imposing steep increases), and cream-skimming (accepting only the very best risks). See also *biased selection*.

MEWAs (multiple employer welfare associations). See *purchasing cooperatives*.

Moral hazard. The market distortion that results from the tendency of insurance to increase the risk that is insured against, on account of subscribers' lowered incentive to guard against the loss. Measures to avoid moral hazard in health insurance include imposing deductibles and copayments and setting limits on covered benefits.

Portability. The condition of insurance that allows subscribers to switch employers or insurers without a gap in coverage. Designed to avoid job lock, which occurs when workers are deterred from switching jobs by the threatened loss of health benefits that results from waiting periods and *preexisting condition exclusions* imposed by the new insurer.

Preexisting condition exclusion. The refusal to cover for a defined period (sometimes forever) those medical conditions that existed at enrollment or during a defined prior period. Intended to counteract *adverse selection*, which occurs when subscribers choose to enroll only when they are sick.

Purchasing cooperative. A device to increase economies of scale and purchasing power for individual and small-group insurance.

99

Also known as a health alliance or a health insurance purchasing cooperative (HIPC). A purchasing cooperative can be governmental, private, or quasi-governmental. Many now exist under the name of multiple employer welfare associations (MEWAs), sponsored by business organizations. Purchasing cooperatives can be voluntary or mandatory, and they can be selective or inclusive. Voluntary cooperatives allow purchasers to buy elsewhere in the market. Selective cooperatives choose which insurers to include based on competitive bids, rather than including all willing insurers.

Rating bands. A method to compress the variation in risk-rated insurance premiums so that insurance remains affordable for higher-risk subscribers. Typically, insurers are allowed to create separate rate bands for different locations and demographic classes, as well as for different *blocks of business*. Within each band, rates may vary only according to prescribed factors and within a set width, such as plus or minus 25 percent based on health risk and 15 percent based on industry classification. Often, however, no limit is set on how much variation can exist among bands.

Reinsurance. Insurance for insurers. The initial insurer cedes a portion of its risk to the reinsurer in exchange for a reinsurance premium. Various forms of reinsurance exist. Private reinsurance allows insurers to purchase stop-loss coverage for their entire block of business. This conventional form of reinsurance takes effect only at a very high (multibillion dollar) level, and the ceding carrier pays the entire reinsurance premium. The quasi-governmental reinsurance mechanism that is part of small-group market reforms differs in several respects. It allows insurers to reinsure individual high-risk subscribers selectively; for these cases, most of the risk is ceded, and the ceding carrier pays only a portion of the reinsurance cost, with the excess costs being assessed proportionately against all insurers in the market. Retrospective reinsurance is a hybrid: like private reinsurance, it is a high-level stop-loss form of reinsurance; like the small-group proposals, it covers selected cases rather than a block of business.

Risk adjustment. A process for compensating insurers for differences in the total risk of their pools of subscribers. The purpose is to lessen the need for risk rating or the incentives for risk selection. Insurers with low-risk pools contribute to, and high-risk insurers draw from, a transfer fund in proportion to their risk differential from the market mean and in proportion to their size. Risk measures can be based on demographics, health status, past treatment, or previous costs. These are prospective methods, which seek to predict future costs based on past evidence. For retrospective risk adjustment, see *reinsurance*.

Variance. A type of risk expressed as the statistical concept that the calculated odds of an event will not bear out in actual experience. An example is a coin toss. The primary odds of flipping heads or tails are 50-50. For any actual series of flips, however, there is a good chance they will not come out precisely as predicted. Variance is this secondary risk. See also *law of large numbers*.

Index

About the Author

MARK A. HALL is a professor of law and public health at Wake Forest University School of Law and Bowman Gray School of Medicine and an associate in management at the Babcock School of Management, all located in Winston-Salem, North Carolina. The author has also completed a Robert Wood Johnson Foundation Health Finance Fellowship at Johns Hopkins University. He specializes in health care law and public policy, with a focus on economic, regulatory, and corporate issues. His present research interests include health care rationing, integrated delivery systems, and insurance market reform.

Board of Trustees

Paul F. Oreffice, *Chairman*
Former Chairman
Dow Chemical Co.

Wilson H. Taylor, *Vice Chairman*
Chairman and CEO
CIGNA Corporation

Tully M. Friedman, *Treasurer*
Hellman & Friedman

Edwin L. Artzt
Chairman and CEO
The Procter & Gamble
  Company

Joseph A. Cannon
Chairman and CEO
Geneva Steel Company

Raymond E. Cartledge
Chairman and CEO
Union Camp Corporation

Albert J. Costello
Chairman and CEO
American Cyanamid Company

Christopher C. DeMuth
President
American Enterprise Institute

Malcolm S. Forbes, Jr.
President and CEO
Forbes Inc.

Christopher B. Galvin
President and Chief Operating Officer
Motorola, Inc.

Robert F. Greenhill
Chairman and CEO
Smith Barney Shearson

M. Douglas Ivester
President
Coca-Cola USA

James W. Kinnear
Former President and CEO
Texaco Incorporated

Bruce Kovner
Chairman
Caxton Corporation

Craig O. McCaw
Chairman and CEO
McCaw Cellular Communications, Inc.

The American Enterprise Institute for Public Policy Research

Founded in 1943, AEI is a nonpartisan, nonprofit, research and educational organization based in Washington, D.C. The Institute sponsors research, conducts seminars and conferences, and publishes books and periodicals.

AEI's research is carried out under three major programs: Economic Policy Studies; Foreign Policy and Defense Studies; and Social and Political Studies. The resident scholars and fellows listed in these pages are part of a network that also includes ninety adjunct scholars at leading universities throughout the United States and in several foreign countries.

The views expressed in AEI publications are those of the authors and do not necessarily reflect the views of the staff, advisory panels, officers, or trustees.

Paul F. O'Neill
Chairman and CEO
Aluminum Company of America

George R. Roberts
Kohlberg Kravis Roberts & Co.

John W. Rowe
President and CEO
New England Electric System

Edward B. Rust, Jr.
Chairman, President, and CEO
State Farm Mutual Automobile
  Insurance Company

Paul G. Stern
Forstmann Little & Co.

Randall L. Tobias
Chairman and CEO
Eli Lilly and Company

Henry Wendt
Former Chairman
SmithKline Beecham

James Q. Wilson
James A. Collins Professor
  of Management
University of California
  at Los Angeles

Charles Wohlstetter
Vice Chairman
GTE Corporation

Officers

Christopher C. DeMuth
President

David B. Gerson
Executive Vice President

Council of Academic Advisers

James Q. Wilson, *Chairman*
James A. Collins Professor
  of Management
University of California
  at Los Angeles

Donald C. Hellmann
Professor of Political Science and
  International Studies
University of Washington

Gertrude Himmelfarb
Distinguished Professor of History
  Emeritus
City University of New York

Samuel P. Huntington
Eaton Professor of the
  Science of Government
Harvard University

D. Gale Johnson
Eliakim Hastings Moore
  Distinguished Service Professor
  of Economics Emeritus
University of Chicago

William M. Landes
Clifton R. Musser Professor of
  Economics
University of Chicago Law School

Glenn C. Loury
Department of Economics
Boston University

Sam Peltzman
Sears Roebuck Professor of Economics
  and Financial Services
University of Chicago
  Graduate School of Business

Nelson W. Polsby
Professor of Political Science
University of California at Berkeley

Murray L. Weidenbaum
Mallinckrodt Distinguished
  University Professor
Washington University

Research Staff

Leon Aron
E. L. Wiegand Fellow

Claude E. Barfield
Resident Scholar; Director, Science
  and Technology Policy Studies

Cynthia A. Beltz
Research Fellow

Walter Berns
Adjunct Scholar

Douglas J. Besharov
Resident Scholar

Jagdish Bhagwati
Visiting Scholar

Robert H. Bork
John M. Olin Scholar in Legal Studies

Michael Boskin
Visiting Scholar

Karlyn Bowman
Resident Fellow; Editor,
  The American Enterprise

Dick B. Cheney
Senior Fellow

Lynne V. Cheney
W.H. Brady, Jr., Distinguished Fellow

Dinesh D'Souza
John M. Olin Research Fellow

Nicholas N. Eberstadt
Visiting Scholar

Mark Falcoff
Resident Scholar

Gerald R. Ford
Distinguished Fellow

Murray F. Foss
Visiting Scholar

Suzanne Garment
Resident Scholar

Jeffrey Gedmin
Research Fellow

Patrick Glynn
Resident Scholar

Robert A. Goldwin
Resident Scholar

Gottfried Haberler
Resident Scholar

Robert W. Hahn
Resident Scholar

Robert B. Helms
Resident Scholar; Director, Health
  Policy Studies

Jeane J. Kirkpatrick
Senior Fellow; Director, Foreign and
  Defense Policy Studies

Marvin H. Kosters
Resident Scholar; Director,
  Economic Policy Studies

Irving Kristol
John M. Olin Distinguished Fellow

Dana Lane
Director of Publications

Michael A. Ledeen
Resident Scholar

James Lilley
Resident Fellow; Director, Asian
  Studies Program

Chong-Pin Lin
Resident Scholar; Associate Director,
  Asian Studies Program

John H. Makin
Resident Scholar; Director, Fiscal
  Policy Studies

Allan H. Meltzer
Visiting Scholar

Joshua Muravchik
Resident Scholar

Charles Murray
Bradley Fellow

Michael Novak
George F. Jewett Scholar in Religion,
  Philosophy, and Public Policy;
  Director, Social and
  Political Studies

Norman J. Ornstein
Resident Scholar

Richard N. Perle
Resident Fellow

William Schneider
Resident Fellow

William Shew
Visiting Scholar

J. Gregory Sidak
Resident Scholar

Herbert Stein
Senior Fellow

Irwin M. Stelzer
Resident Scholar; Director, Regulatory
  Policy Studies

W. Allen Wallis
Resident Scholar

Ben J. Wattenberg
Senior Fellow

Carolyn L. Weaver
Resident Scholar; Director, Social
  Security and Pension Studies

A Note on the Book

This book was edited by Ann Petty of the AEI Press.
The text was set in Palatino, a typeface designed by
the twentieth-century Swiss designer Hermann Zapf.
Coghill Composition Company of Richmond, Virginia,
set the type, and Maple-Vail Book Manufacturing Group,
of York, Pennsylvania, printed and bound the book,
using permanent acid-free paper.

The AEI Press is the publisher for the American Enterprise Institute for Public Policy Research, 1150 17th Street, N.W., Washington, D.C. 20036; *Christopher C. DeMuth*, publisher; *Dana Lane*, director; *Ann Petty*, editor; *Cheryl Weissman*, editor; *Lisa Roman*, editorial assistant (rights and permissions).